THE DUKE OF
BEAUFORT

Memoirs

THE DUKE OF
BEAUFORT

Memoirs

Country Life Books

Published by Country Life Books
Holman House, 95 Sheen Road, Richmond upon Thames,
Surrey, TW9 1YJ
and distributed for them by
The Hamlyn Publishing Group Limited
London · New York · Sydney · Toronto
Astronaut House, Feltham, Middlesex, England

First published 1981

ISBN 0 600 31574 6

Set in 11pt Palatino
Set, printed and bound in Great Britain by
Fakenham Press Limited, Fakenham, Norfolk

DEDICATION

I dedicate this book of memoirs which tells a little of the story of Badminton and my forebears to those who will come after – to my cousin David Somerset and to all his family.

Mutare vel timere sperno
(I scorn to change or to fear)

AUTHOR'S NOTE

I want to place on record my grateful thanks to Gloria Cottesloe who has spent the last couple of years or more in helping me to collect together and place on paper all the anecdotes that have resulted in this book. Without her professional help, advice and the systematic thoroughness with which she has not only encouraged my memory, but also sifted all the material that exists, I would not have been able to tell the story of my own life and a little about my ancestors, placing it all on record for posterity.

CONTENTS

LIST OF ILLUSTRATIONS

28 *With H.M. the Queen on Coronation Day. In the Royal Procession it was my duty and privilege to ride immediately behind my Monarch's coach.*

29 *Representing King George VI at Lloyd George's Memorial Service, 10 April 1945. During the forty years or so that I was Master of the Horse I frequently represented the Sovereign on official occasions both here and abroad.*

30 *With me are (l. to r.) Mary, Mrs Roosevelt, Queen Mary, The Princess Royal. The date was 4 November 1942.*

31 *One of Queen Mary's 'Wooding Squads' during the Second World War.*

32 *The Queen sometimes likes to ride when she visits Badminton. This occasion was in April 1959.*

33 *Members of the Royal Family at the Three-Day Event in 1962. I wonder if Princess Anne already had ideas of competing at Badminton.*

34 *We always have a special service in the Church during the Three-Day Event, when we generally invite a Bishop to preach.*

35 *With some of my young hound bitches.*

36 *With some of my red deer stags that are standing by the Park Pond, November 1980.*

INTRODUCTION

In writing this book of memoirs, my idea has been not only to talk about my own life, but to tell the story of Badminton and something about my ancestors.

Heredity and environment have certainly been equally responsible for making me the man I am. Badminton has been the background to my life, and the House, the estates and the position to which I was born have necessarily provided a discipline within which the pattern of my life has been formed.

My entry in the reference books sounds formidable, but serves to give an idea of the hereditary offices I hold and the duties they bring with them.

The 10th Duke of Beaufort (Sir Henry Hugh Arthur FitzRoy Somerset, K.G., P.C., G.C.V.O.), Marquess and Earl of Worcester, Lord Botetourt, Lord Herbert of Herbert and Lord Herbert of Raglan, Chepstow and Gower, Lord Lieutenant and Customs Rotulorum of Bristol and Gloucestershire, Lord High Steward of Bristol, Gloucester and Tewkesbury, Hereditary Keeper of Raglan Castle, Master of the Horse from 1936 to 1977, Steward of Tewkesbury from 1948, elected Chancellor of Bristol University 1965, K.St.J., *educ.* Eton, and R.M.C., (Sandhurst), late Royal Horse Guards, Hon. Col. 21st (Royal Gloucester Hussars) Armoured Car Co. from 1926, has Grand Cross of Legion of Honour; created G.C.V.O. 1 Jan. 1930, sworn of the Privy Council of Great Britain 27 Oct. 1936 and created K.G. 11 May, 1937; received Royal Victorian Chain 1953; b. 4 April, 1900; s. his father as

10th Duke 1924; m. 14 June, 1923 Lady Mary Cambridge, elder dau. of 1st Marquess of Cambridge.

In this book I explain the duties of many of these offices and how it comes about that I bear so many titles. I would like to point out that I am particularly proud to have inherited the High Stewardship of Bristol, Gloucester and Tewkesbury. In a yellowing newspaper cutting that I have saved, a journalist wrote:

> ... It is an office regarded in high honour; it carries neither emoluments nor duties beyond the maintenance of the dignity of the position.

It is, in fact, an office whereby should there be any disagreement at the Quarter Sessions, I act *in loco Rex* in a judiciary capacity, it being my privilege to cast the deciding vote.

My position as Lord Lieutenant of Bristol and of Gloucestershire also carried no emoluments, but there were certainly many duties and considerable dignity of position. The Lord Lieutenant of a county is the personal representative of the Monarch, for whom he deputises on many occasions; he or she is also required to be present whenever a member of the Royal Family visits the county in an official capacity. Although the duties at times were onerous, I enjoyed them all, and now, when I look back, I realise to the full what an interesting life they have caused me to lead – how many people from all walks of life I have met, and what lovely places I have visited.

During the postal strike a few years ago, I felt very frustrated, as not only was there no post, which gave me an unaccustomed hour of freedom after breakfast, but it was also during the winter months at a time when the weather was so frosty that it was impossible to hunt. So I decided to start some notebooks with various scraps of material – old photographs, newspaper cuttings, favourite poems: all sorts of bits and pieces that I had hoarded over the years.

I rummaged around the house and found a nice big hard-backed notebook with a leather-bound spine and corners, covered with marbled paper bearing a red label that reads: 'Measurement of Roads from Badminton' inscribed in elegant gold lettering – and throughout the book, written in beautiful copper-plate handwriting in black Indian Ink, are lists of those measurements. This was just the sort of thing I wanted, so I began then and there with an aerial photograph of Badminton taken in July 1930, which shows quite clearly the circular cricket pitch in front of the north side of the house where my father used to entertain the giants of cricket and I in my turn provided some exciting matches with teams drawn from the Gloucestershire cricketers of the 1920s and 1930s.

Next there comes a snapshot of the north side of the house taken by the Duke of Edinburgh with a note on its back saying: 'In case you forget where you belong.' Following this is the description that I give later in this book of the visit paid to Badminton by Queen Alexandra and her sister, Empress Marie of Russia, together with a couple of photographs neatly captioned as having been taken only a few days earlier of a Meet at the Monument on 28 March 1909. However, on looking on the back, I find the words in my mother's handwriting: 'Hawkesbury Upton March 25th, 1907.'

I have included extracts from my notebooks throughout this book, because I think that it is from such random collections that people are able to form an idea of what a man is really like.

Although I have led a life of privilege, that privilege has brought with it certain responsibilities and obligations, and these I have tried to fulfil to the best of my ability. Whether or not I have been successful will no doubt be judged by historians in later years. I only hope that they will be as kind to me as they have been to my ancestors.

CHAPTER ONE

THE BEGINNING

It was a bright and sunny morning in early April. The year was
1900, and Queen Victoria was still on the throne. All the birds
were singing merrily in the trees and hedgerows as the 9th Duke
of Beaufort rode on to a Meet of his foxhounds. It was about a
quarter past ten, and he was on his way to Burton, a hamlet that
lies only a few miles to the south of his Gloucestershire home,
Badminton.

Although he was never a particularly talkative man with his
staff, especially before hunting, this spring morning the Duke
was even quieter and more thoughtful than usual, though his
huntsman, Will Dale, and the two whippers-in did not think
there was anything particularly strange either in his behaviour
or in his manner. To tell you the truth, amazing though it would
have seemed to that trio of men in the green plush coats of the
Badminton outdoor servants, and indeed unbelievable to those
who knew the Duke well, his mind was not on hunting at all.

For once in his life he was not very happy to be in the saddle
and – what is even more startling – I am sure he would far rather
have been in the centre of London instead of making his way
across the invisible line that divides Gloucestershire from Wiltshire on his way to a Meet of his hounds with the prospect of a
day's hunting ahead.

There is little doubt that his whole mind was centred on what
had been happening during the previous twenty-four hours at
No. 19 Curzon Street, Mayfair, for early that morning a breath-
less messenger had arrived at Badminton House with a telegram. Now it was the contents of the small yellow envelope that
his valet had brought to him earlier while he was pulling on his
boots that were totally occupying his thoughts to the exclusion
of all else.

A Meet of the Duke of Beaufort's hounds at Burton in April was not a particularly fashionable one, as the hill country round Castle Coombe did not attract very many horsemen at that time of year, for by then most of the members of the hunt would have turned their hunters away for the summer, and the horses would be being roughed-off in preparation for their summer rest out at grass.

After waiting a few minutes and exchanging a word or two with somebody who had some information that he wanted to pass on, the Duke glanced at his watch. It was time to make a move. Before giving his usual signal to the huntsman, who was watching him carefully, he doffed his hat – he only wore a hunting cap when he was hunting hounds himself – and lifting up his hand a moment for silence, he addressed the small assembly of riders and people on foot.

> 'Before we go off to draw, I thought you would like
> to know that early this morning my wife gave birth to a
> son.'

A moment or two of silence followed this thrilling piece of news while they all digested its import. Then Will Dale, the huntsman, plucked up his courage and rather hesitantly said:

> 'May we give three cheers, Your Grace?'
> The reply he had was abrupt and to the point:
> 'Certainly not! You might frighten the hounds.'

So saying, the Duke rammed on his hat again, and with a quick nod to the crimson-faced Will, he wheeled his horse round and beckoned to the Field to follow him to the first draw.

So that is how the news of my arrival was conveyed to the world at large!

My father did not marry until comparatively late in life, for he was forty-eight years of age when he chose for his bride a young widow, who had herself been born and bred in Gloucestershire. Her maiden name was Louise Harford, and she had lived as a girl at Oldown, Almondsbury, not very many miles from Badminton. When she was scarcely out of the schoolroom, she had married Baron Carlo de Tuyll (his was a Dutch title, though he lived in England) and before she was twenty-one she had borne him two sons in quick succession. However, their happiness

1. *In my mother's arms on the day of my christening,
with my two sisters, Diana and Blanche, close by.*

2. *I am holding the whip, Blanche is driving and Diana is the passenger. The donkey was called Neddy and he lived until he was well over 40 years old.*

3. *Blanche, Fred Matthews, my father, Diana, the stud-groom, Dyer, a temporary groom and me – riding Neddy.*

was not destined to last, for only a few brief years later, the young couple were in a terrible railway accident in America, and although she herself was not hurt, she had seen her husband killed before her very eyes. The dreadful shock turned her beautiful dark hair quite white overnight: that is the sort of thing you read about in storybooks, and it hardly ever seems to happen in real life, but I can assure you that it was true in my mother's case.

After that tragic bereavement, she returned to England and bought a pleasant house at Horton, which lies halfway between her old home and Badminton, and just down the road from Petty France, the house where one of her brothers lived with his wife and children. Her intention was to bring up her two little boys near to her family, this being natural enough, for she was still quite young, and probably felt very much alone in the world, especially as most of her husband's relations lived in Holland.

I imagine that once the immediate grief and bitterness of her cruel loss had worn off, and by the time she had settled herself down into as normal a way of life as possible, it must surely have crossed her mind occasionally that one day she might marry for a second time. What I am absolutely certain never entered her head for a moment was the fact that she was destined to become Duchess of Beaufort.

Meanwhile, at Badminton, a few miles away, my grandfather was seventy years of age and not enjoying the best of health, so I dare say he was bringing considerable pressure to bear on his eldest son to marry, settle down and raise a family of his own at Badminton. I am sure that this must have been the dearest wish of the old man, for, in common with everyone who is born to great estates, he must have been anxious to see the inheritance secured, preferably through his eldest son.

Naturally by the time he was going on for fifty, my father must have had several romantic adventures, but evidently he had never loved a woman sufficiently to ask her to be his wife; or perhaps the truth of the matter is that he had never loved anyone who was free to marry him. However, even though I am sure he would have respected his father's wishes and would have pleased him if he could, I am equally certain that, however urgently a suit was pressed, my father would never have allowed himself to be persuaded into a marriage of convenience with someone he did not love with all his heart. I expect he had seen and made a mental note of my mother when she came out in the hunting field, for she was extremely beautiful and an

3

elegant horsewoman, so she was not likely to have gone unnoticed, and doubtless he was attracted to her; even though he may have found himself a little swayed by his father's obviously urgent wishes when the courtship began, I am absolutely convinced that the union of my parents was a love match. They were so obviously devoted to one another, and all through my youth they seemed to me to be in complete harmony.

In point of fact, there was an extremely sound basis for their marriage on several grounds, quite apart from their evidently having fallen deeply in love with one another, for not only did they share a love of hunting, but also my mother, being a Gloucestershire girl, liked and got on well with all my father's closest friends. In addition, she had had experience in running her own household, and therefore knew full well what would be expected of her should she marry my father and eventually go to live at Badminton House. Competent direction from above is essential to ensure the smooth running of a great household, however many servants there may be. Another factor, too, that may unconsciously have governed my father's choice is that by the time he was forty-eight years old and set in his ways, I am sure he would have had no desire to start taming a flighty young girl. With all the wisdom of hindsight, I feel certain that my parents were made for one another.

Their wedding took place quietly on 9 October 1895 in the Church that adjoins the House at Badminton. While I can find no record of the actual place they went to for their honeymoon, and alas it never occurred to me to ask them when they were still alive, what I do know for certain is that it only lasted for two brief days. Why was this, you will ask? Because of the cub-hunting, of course! Whatever else? I cannot see many brides standing for that sort of thing nowadays!

Eighteen months later, in April 1897, my elder sister, Blanche was born. She was most suitably named, for Blanche is a name that has appeared in our family records for nearly five hundred years, ever since John of Gaunt, Duke of Lancaster and fourth son of Edward III, founded our family. He was known as 'Gaunt' because he was born in Ghent in the Low Countries during the exile of his father. His first wife, whom he loved dearly, was called Blanche of Lancaster; after she died, even though he soon married Constance of Castile, the woman who actually took Blanche's place in his affections was Katharine, wife of Sir Hugh Swynford and sister-in-law of Chaucer. She became his acknowledged mistress, what today I suppose would be called a common-law-wife, and bore him four children. These children were eventually legitimised by Act of Parliament on condition that no member of the family should make a claim to the throne.

It is rather ironical to find that in 1914 every reigning sovereign in Europe, with the sole exception of the King of Spain, could trace their descent from John of Gaunt and Katharine Swynford! Although we Somersets have always been in a very strong position to make a claim to the throne of England, I can solemnly assure you that no such claim has ever been contemplated. My family have always been among the most loyal subjects of our Monarch – and I can safely say that there will be no Civil War on my account!

Having made that quite clear, I must say that we are naturally very proud of our Plantagenet blood and descent, and perhaps the more so when one reads the following passage from a letter written some years ago to the Editor of *The Times* by Lord Mersey:

> The Plantagenets, indeed, were nearly all men of real character and personality . . . They were a handsome, virile, courageous, intellectual and masterful race; great fighters, builders and hunters – their flag flying over Badminton still attests the continuity of the last trait . . .

Although my mother must have been thrilled to have her first little daughter – after all, did she not already have two sons of her own? – I am equally certain that her natural joy must have been tinged with a little regret, for she would have known very well how much her husband, and not only he, but her father-in-law, the old Duke, were longing for the birth of a son and eventual heir to Badminton and the great estates that go with it both in England and in Wales, and all that they stood for. The baby girl thrived and was very much loved by her parents and, perhaps, more surprisingly, idolised by her grandfather. This goes to show, I think, what a sweet nature he must have had, for he might well have been so disappointed that she was not a boy that he could easily have turned against her, or at any rate, have taken little or no interest in her. In a biography about him by T. F. Dale, *The Eighth Duke of Beaufort and the Badminton Hunt*, written in true Victorian style, there occurs the following little passage which I find most moving:

... But as the days of the Duke grew to a close, a still greater consolation came to him. He was spared to see the marriage of his eldest son in 1895 ... The Duke had always loved children, and they, as their custom is, had returned his affection. When his eldest grand-daughter was born, he poured out upon her the affection he had given to his own daughter, of whose birth he speaks so tenderly in his diary. He loved the little grand-daughter intensely, and her welfare was his most absorbing thought during the last two years of his life.

A fact that I think must surely have had a great bearing on my grandfather's great love for my sister was that his only and much-loved daughter, Blanche, who married the Marquess of Waterford as his second wife, had died after a lingering illness only a few weeks before my sister, her namesake, was born.

The biographer went on:

... Could he have been spared to see the birth of the heir to the ancient name which took place in 1900, it would have rejoiced him.

Alas, that was not to be, for the very next year my mother gave birth to a second daughter, this child being christened Diana, the name of the Goddess of the Chase being an obvious choice for a girl in a family like ours with such a hunting tradition.

After the arrival of these two little daughters, I think it is small wonder that when they were expecting their third child a year or so later, my father, absolutely convinced that this baby would also turn out to be a girl, elected to stay behind at Badminton to finish the hunting season, while my mother went to London alone as the time of her accouchement drew near.

This must have been the one time in his life when my father was genuinely pleased to be proved wrong. However emphatic had been his belief that I would prove to be another daughter – and however casual his demeanour had been at the Meet of his hounds at Burton – the fact is that he was genuinely overjoyed when I eventually put in my appearance during the early hours of Monday, 4 April 1900. I dare say that his first reaction was one of stunned disbelief, and it probably took some time for the full awareness of what had happened to penetrate his mind.

I was born, as are all the eldest sons born to the Dukes of

Beaufort, to the courtesy title of the Marquess of Worcester, and I like to remember that for my first ten months I was a Victorian, for that great Queen did not die until 22 January the following year, when the whole country plunged into deep mourning, and there was great sadness throughout the lands. The fact that I was born in 1900 means that I have lived during six reigns – and as I am happy and honoured to count myself as among the many friends of the present Prince of Wales, heir to the throne, I do hope that I shall live long enough to know his children.

Although my official name, therefore, was the Marquess of Worcester until I succeeded my father and became the Duke of Beaufort, Worcester was also the name by which my father was known by all his friends until the day of his death. I was christened Henry Hugh Arthur FitzRoy, though I was known in the family and at school as Harry (sometimes when my school-friends wanted to get a rise out of me they would call me Sauce!) and as far as I can remember my mother always called me 'darling' and the staff at Badminton, 'Master Worcester' or 'My Lord'.

When I was eleven I acquired a new name when my father gave me a pack of harriers for my birthday. People would come up to me and say: 'Good morning, Master. Where are you going to draw today?' It was from that little joke that the name by which I have been called ever since derives, for everyone now calls me 'Master', and it is a name that I both like and am proud to have.

The time of my birth was a time of strife in the world, for the Boxer Rebellion and the Boer War occupied not only the columns of the newspapers, but also the minds of the people as a whole, and out in the Far East, the Russo–Japanese War was brewing. However, in so far as an estate like Badminton was concerned, those early years of the century were still times of plenty. Income tax was ridiculously low compared with the crippling sums we are called upon to pay nowadays – but on the very day of my birth it went up from sevenpence to eightpence in the pound! However ridiculous that sum sounds to us in these days of inflation and high taxation, believe me, eighty years ago it caused the greatest concern, for it was felt to be an encroachment on civil liberty that people should be called upon to dip into their pockets in such a way. Doubtless some economies were effected for a short time in all households, whether great or small, and I am told that in one noble family, the butler was sent out to buy a set of table-napkin rings, so that instead of everyone having a clean napkin at every meal as had hitherto always been the custom, only one per person was henceforward to be provided each day. In their naivety, the family fully expected that such a revolutionary step would quickly restore their fortunes!

However, I don't for a moment think that many economies were made that summer of 1900 at Badminton, for there were great celebrations all round to welcome me into the world, and while, even then, such parties must have cost a lot of money, I am sure my father felt that it was money well spent.

When I was a child, we, in common with most Edwardian great houses, had what in many households would have been called a Steward, but we called him the Head Butler. Perhaps that was because his name was David Head! He was in full charge of the organisation of the whole of the male side of the indoor staff, and beneath him, he had an Under butler, whose concern was the day-to-day duties of the valets and the footmen.

There were eight young footmen, and I can remember when in the evenings they discarded their daytime uniform, and were powdered and dressed in the family blue livery, with smart blue and buff striped waistcoats, those family colours of ours echoing the old Lancastrian ones of azure and gold. Nowadays in these chilly times of domestic austerity, powdered and liveried footmen are an anachronistic sight only to be seen on the stage in a pantomime, or perhaps on the screen of the cinema or television in one of those popular Edwardian films so beloved of the general public – perhaps because they evoke nostalgic dreams of a way of life that will never return.

Lower down the scale at Badminton came a platoon of men who did all the odd jobs about the place, such as cleaning the windows, carrying the coal, washing the floors and lighting the lamps. Then came the page-boys who, hoping one day to graduate as footmen, ran busily about the house and grounds, taking and bringing back messages and making themselves generally useful. We even employed a man whose sole task it was to see that the clocks were in working order, to wind them regularly and make sure they all told the right time; and there was another whose job in life was to look after all the lamps and candles.

The female side of the staff was headed by the Housekeeper, who, even if unmarried, in common with many female cooks in those days, was often given the honorary title of 'Mrs' – no nonsense like Ms then! She was responsible not only for all the work and welfare of the female staff, but also for seeing that provisions were laid in for the whole household, and for the supervision of the linen and of the laundry – which was done in a building opposite to the west entrance to the house. She was also in charge of the still-room where her maids cooked all the cakes, bottled the fruit that was grown in the garden and turned out hundreds of pots of jam and marmalade.

When I was a little boy, for several years the actual kitchens were ruled over by the French Chef, Grand-Jean; it was he who produced the delicious meals that we ate with great relish and enormous appetites.

There was a bevy of female staff then, under the jurisdiction of the Housekeeper: scullery maids, housemaids, parlour maids, ladies' maids, together forming a veritable army of women; but it seemed like an invisible army, for most of the actual housework was done in the early hours of the morning when we were all still asleep. Should one of the housemaids hear a member of the family or one of the guests approaching when she was going about her duties, she would scuttle like a mouse into the wainscoting, slipping through one of the numerous little doors all over the house that lead to a labyrinth of little passages and stairways, which were the joy of my life when I was small and the weather was too bad for me to go out. Badminton House is a child's dream for playing hide-and-seek. I guarantee that no one would ever find me if I chose to hide myself away.

The housemaids were so coy about being seen, having been adjured from their earliest days of service to disappear in this way, that when we had our fire practices which happened from time to time, they would throw their skirts over their heads and show their voluminous beribboned white drawers rather than catch a glimpse of their blushing faces!

Outside the house, the man in charge was called the Clerk of the Works, and he was responsible for the eighteen gardeners who worked under the Head Gardener, and all the other outside staff – their livery colour traditionally being green. Green was also the livery colour of the hunt servants at the kennels who consisted of the huntsman with his two whippers-in and three kennelmen. The stables were under the authority of the stud-groom who had a feeder and forty-two strappers working under him; in addition there was a saddler, and a blacksmith. As that was well before the advent of the internal combustion machine there had to be, of course, a Head Coachman and a Second

Coachman. Later on when my father bought a Panhard, he employed a French chauffeur about whom I will tell you further on in this book.

As anything from twelve-and-sixpence (62½p.) up to twenty-five shillings (£1.25p.) a week was considered a good wage for agricultural workers in the early years of this century, it is very difficult to compare those figures with what we have to pay men nowadays, when the minimum agricultural wage is something in the region of £60 a week; if we employ women for outside work, they have to be paid the same rates as men, regardless of the fact that they cannot be expected to have the same strength, even though they often have more stamina.

Although the wages seem very low when compared with those paid nowadays, our servants at Badminton benefited in many other ways. Long service is, and always has been, rewarded by continuing the provision of accommodation after retirement, and widows are never left without a roof over their heads. They are all entitled to free fuel in the form of wood from the Park, and milk is free to those working with the dairy herds, of which we have three – two shorthorn herds and a Jersey herd, the latter having recently been brought to Badminton from West Kington where they were kept for many years.

When I was young, we even ran our own form of health service, for every Sunday at a quarter to two, a dogcart would draw up at the door, and out would jump Dr Mellish who would first have luncheon with us, and afterwards he held a sort of surgery in the house, when anybody on the Estate could attend if there was something wrong with them. This service was free to them, but my father paid Dr Mellish £250 a year, which was quite a lot of money in those days. I remember the doctor sometimes arrived a little late, for he was very keen on cock-fighting and, when he was on his way to Badminton, he would often drop off some of the fighting cocks that he had bred at farms or pubs on the way where a cock-fighting session was going to be held the following week.

Although I spent a good deal of time in the stables throughout my youth, I did not often have occasion to go into the kitchen regions, though I can remember being called down to stir the Christmas pudding and to make my wish. However, I was always on good terms with most of the younger members of the domestic staff, and I have been fortunate enough to inherit both my father and my grandfather's capacity for making friends easily, and then, once having made them, I keep them. I think I am in a very fortunate position, for I have many friends, and I don't think I have any enemies – except perhaps people who are anti-field sports and possibly belong to the League Against Cruel Sports.

Every morning after breakfast, my mother would make her way to her sitting-room. This is a nice room that we now use as a dining-room when the house is open to the public in the summer months; it lies off the corridor that leads directly to the Church. When she had seated herself at her desk, she would pull a bell-rope, and a minute or two later the French Chef, Grand-Jean, Chef d'Honneur, would come to be interviewed. Together they would discuss the menus for that day, and perhaps make plans for the future if there were a large number of people coming to stay, or if there were a very special dinner party to arrange

When they had finished their business, and my mother was satisfied that, whatever else may happen, the food would still appear, she would pull another bell-rope which was connected by a complicated system of wires and pulleys (some of which are still to be seen in the passage that we habitually use on our way to the main part of the house, marked 'His Grace's Valet' and so on) to summon the Housekeeper. Down she would come hastily, for she had been waiting for the sound of the bell in the linen-room – a room lined with cupboards that contained all the linen, spare blankets, towels, candles, soap and so on, everything in fact that was necessary to contribute to the smooth running of a great household. The Housekeeper always carried the keys to all those cupboards round her waist on a silver châtelaine, and she guarded them as if they were the Holy Grail itself.

When my mother had finished her morning session with the Housekeeper, having discussed all the affairs of the still-room and any other urgent matters that might have arisen concerning the welfare or conduct of the female staff, it was then the turn of the Head Butler. He would be told by my mother how many guests to expect for luncheon and for dinner, who they were and what time they would be arriving. If people were coming to stay for a night or two, my mother would also pass on to him any personal little idiosyncrasies known to her should they not have stayed at Badminton before. Out would come David Head's valuable little notebook in which he kept a record of all the personal things that he needed to remember about our guests, many of whom were habitual visitors, coming time after time and paying seasonal visits for one reason or another. Perhaps Sir James suffered from gout and therefore needed an extra pillow in the bedroom on which to rest his leg, or maybe Lady something-or-other hated draughts and disliked finding the windows open when she arrived. It is very welcoming when I visit other people's houses to find that my own particular tastes have been catered for. You then feel that people really care, for we all have our personal little likes and dislikes.

When he had been told how many people were expected for dinner that night, David Head would then know how much champagne he should bring up from the cellar, for my father, like his father before him, had nothing else served at his table. He always had his own bottle put in front of him, and similarly, every male guest would find a bottle in front of his place when he came into dinner. At the end of the meal, if any of the bottles were left unfinished, then my father would go round and tip them up into his glass, quaffing the lot. My grandfather, on the other hand, even though he always had champagne served at his table, never drank it himself.

After dinner, before joining the ladies in the drawing-room, my father would offer his male guests a glass or two of vintage Madeira of which he was a connoisseur and of which he would have nothing but the best in his cellar. This I discovered to my eventual cost when he died, for when the people came to do a valuation for probate, I found that I was required to pay heavy duty on all the bottles of Madeira that were left in the cellar. How I wished I had drunk it all myself before the valuers appeared on the scene!

Should my mother intend during the course of the day to leave Badminton to drive, say, to Bath, or to visit friends in a neighbouring village, then she would tell the Head Butler, who in turn would inform the relevant gate-keepers, so that when my mother's brougham – which he also had to order to be at the door on time – came into sight, she would find a green liveried man waiting with his gate wide open, and he would doff his top-hat to her as the carriage swept past.

My earliest memories are of waking in the morning to the mournful sound of the baying of my father's hounds in the kennels which lie a quarter of a mile away. I have never tired of that sound, and am glad that the nursery suite is on that side of the house. While I was sleepily opening my eyes, I would hear a series of thuds as Toghill, who was responsible for the fires throughout the house, put down some kindling and scuttles of coal for the nursery fires at the top of the stairs, so that by the time we appeared for breakfast there was a good blaze in the day nursery grate. There were open fires in all the bedrooms when I was a child, and I often remember how lovely it was to go to sleep with the reassuring reflection of the flames flickering on the ceiling making all sorts of patterns and shapes. What a comforting sight it was, and what a lot the modern child misses to my mind, in spite of the so-called modern conveniences of electricity and central heating.

By the time I was fully awake, I would be aware of my Nanny up and dressed, moving about the room drawing back the curtains and checking that I and my sisters had had the correct clothes put out for us to wear that morning. I shared my bedroom, which was known as the night nursery, with Nanny Wright, and then with her successor, throughout my earlier years. Another nightly occupant of the room was the nursery dog, a big black poodle called, I regret to say, Sambo. Although he did not sleep on my bed – I don't think Nanny Wright's tolerance would have stretched that far – that lucky dog curled himself up on a sofa in front of the fire. What Nanny Wright thought of this arrangement, I do not know, for she never said anything to me about it, but I imagine that when she first accepted a post in a family like ours, whose whole lives were known to revolve around sport, she must have been well aware of what to expect. Dogs, horses, hounds and the endless talk of hunting and shooting, combined with all the muddy clothes we brought back to her to deal with after our outings – she took it all in her stride.

I really loved Nanny Wright, who played an extremely important part in my most formative years, not that she ever made any attempt either by word or deed to usurp the place that rightfully belonged to my mother. No good children's nurse would ever dream of doing that, for she knows full well that her role in life is to provide an additional prop to a child, and to give her charges extra comfort, love and security, over and above that which naturally comes from their parents. Comfort, love and security to my mind are three of the most important things on which to build the foundations of a young life. Those three benefits do not apply only to young human beings, but equally to hounds and horses.

One Sunday morning – I cannot have been more than four or

five years old – I was sitting as usual with my mother and sisters in the family pew which is in a gallery at the back of our Church. This pew is reached by way of a passage that leads to it directly from the House, a passage that in those days of my early youth seemed to me to be magically revealed when a whole section of what turns out to be sham-bookcase is swung aside. We had just sat down after the choir had filed to their places to the accompaniment of solemn organ music, and there was a short lull before the service began. Idly I played with my leather-bound prayer book and studied a picture of Jesus who, bearing an agonised expression, was wearing His crown-of-thorns. The silence was suddenly and violently broken by a heavy thud. Jumping up on to a footstool so that I could peer over the edge of the pew that normally was far above my head, I saw there below me in the middle of the aisle the crumpled heap of my beloved Nanny Wright lying on the ground. The poor woman had suffered a massive heart attack, and had died on the spot. In many ways, of course, it was the best end for her, as it is for anyone who is fortunate enough to die like that.

But it was a terrible shock for all of us, and I think that I was perhaps the one who was likely to be most affected, as I was still so very young and so very dependent on her. Subsequently my mother found it difficult to explain to me what had happened couched in terms that would not frighten me even more and cause me to fear that the same thing might happen at any time to another of the people I loved. She told me afterwards that I was very sensible about it, and fortunately accepted readily the theory that Nanny Wright simply couldn't wait to go and live with Jesus. I think it is a fact that children are far less affected by tragedies than grown-ups expect them to be, as they seem to take all sorts of things in their stride, adjusting themselves very quickly to changing circumstances.

I certainly did in this case, as fortunately I had already formed a great attachment for the under-Nurse, Sarah Meadows, and my little voice was to be heard all over the house and garden plaintively wailing: ''Arah-come. 'Arah-come.' I couldn't say my s's properly, and I was always trotting around demanding both Sarah's presence and her full attention. Fortunately she was another very nice woman, and quite capable of taking over Nanny Wright's duties and position in the household straight away, thus causing the nursery routine to continue in its usual comfortable and comforting way. When she eventually left our service, she went to my Harford cousins, four boys who I dare say led her quite a dance, though I am sure she was well able to cope with them.

Each morning at about eight o'clock, the nursery footman would bring up our breakfast from the kitchens which were immediately below us on the west side of the house. This was a good thing, as it meant that the food did not have to travel very far, and was therefore still hot when we sat down to eat it. That was of course long before the days of electric hot-plates – we made do with spirit burners and nightlights – and the only concession of that sort in the nursery was a porridge plate I habitually used which was hollow inside and could be filled with hot water through a little spout at the side that had a screw cap on it. On the plate itself was a picture which I was always anxious to uncover little by little, until its beauty became complete when I had carefully scraped up the last spoonful. I can't even remember now what the picture was; all I remember is that I thought it was lovely.

Suitably bibbed or pinafored, we three children and any guest children who happened to be staying in the house, sat at the nursery table that had been laid with the special silver and china that was kept entirely for nursery use. For our breakfast we had the usual bacon and egg, which came from the pigs and poultry on one of our farms, or perhaps a homemade sausage. This was followed by toast which originated from the last season's wheat crop, piled with butter that had been made on the Estate, honey that came from local beehives, and marmalade made in the still-room. I was rather reluctantly persuaded to swallow a mug of milk, urged on by the only bribe that ever had any effect on me. The cunning Nanny Wright knew full well how much I adored and venerated my father, so she said:

'Drink it up, Master Worcester, and then you'll grow up big and strong just like your father.'

Although I don't think I ever consciously copied my father, it is evident that I modelled myself on him, as is witnessed by the photograph of me as a small boy posing outside the house one morning before going out hunting. With almost identical stance, I am holding my hunting whip with a careful loop made in its thong, in the same way as my father. The only difference is that I have one toe pointing outwards. Perhaps that is because I had just started dancing lessons! Madame Vacani, who, a generation later taught our present Queen to dance, used to come down to Badminton once a week by train and hold a class for local children in the House. I always used to station myself in the back row so that I could sneak out when I heard my father returning from hunting, and find out what sort of day he had had. However, later on, I was to find myself glad that I had had those lessons when I first stepped into the ballrooms as a Sandhurst cadet.

Breakfast and supper were the only meals we habitually had in the nursery, for as a rule we had luncheon in the dining-room downstairs with our mother when she was in. Our father was nearly always out hunting, and sometimes our mother went hunting too. We loved to have our tea downstairs, for by then our father in all probability would have returned; although he only drank a cup of tea himself while we stuffed ourselves with toast, crumpets and cakes, he would regale us with stories of the day's hunting, and I truly think that is how the foundations of my hunting knowledge were laid.

On looking back, it seems that we children saw a great deal more of our parents than most of our contemporaries did of theirs; I think that this must have been a family tradition, because when I study the records I find that the children of the household were generally to be found downstairs, not banished to the nursery wing only to be brought out all clean and tidy for presentation to their mother and father for half an hour after tea.

The 5th Duke's wife, Elizabeth, daughter of Admiral Boscawen, had a serious carriage accident in 1769, which left her with a permanently stiff leg, and she was unable to leave Badminton. Her mother, Mrs Boscawen, suggested in her journal that the fact that so many of the Beaufort babies not only survived but thrived, was the indirect result of this accident, as their mother was able to devote the whole of her attention to them. This is probably true, for in those days long ago, children were left to be brought up by servants, and scarcely ever saw their parents. Happily that was not so in our case.

I am very glad that my parents took the view that their children were to be both seen and heard; otherwise with a much older-than-usual father I might not have had the opportunity to get to know him properly and to imbibe his wisdom and superb know-how in the hunting field. Although naturally I respected my parents, they were also my friends.

When we reached the age of five, our years were divided into terms like a school, though we were always allowed days off for hunting. I like a little piece in a book written about my grandfather, where the biographer (T. F. Dale) said that when he talked to the children they told him:

16

'We are not allowed to hunt more than four times a
week until we reach the age of five years old.'

From that age then, until I was nine years old, I was obliged to
acquire a passing knowledge of the arts of reading, writing and
arithmetic – very little more, I fear – from my sisters' governess,
Miss Marshall. I must admit that I do not remember much about
Miss Marshall, except that to my youthful eyes she seemed to be
a very dull and indoor sort of person. I am sure that she was a
very nice woman, for she and my two sisters seemed to get on
well, and she stayed at Badminton throughout the time they
were being educated. Had she been a more sporting type of
woman, very likely I would have remembered more about her,
but I was much more interested in the mixed pack of terriers and
lurchers that my sisters and I enjoyed hunting in the park, which
in those days stretched for miles right outside the house.

Book-learning never did appeal much to me, though Miss
Marshall evidently must have taught well, for I had no trouble at
all with my work when I went on to my private school, and she
certainly made a good job of the education of my sisters.

When she grew up my younger sister, Diana, wrote and
illustrated two or three books in partnership with Lady Apsley,
the mother of the present Earl Bathurst who was herself, like
both my sisters, a fine horsewoman and extremely knowledgeable about all aspects of horsemanship. Those books were written in a racy, easy style and have stood the test of time. They are
well worth reading, as they are small classics of their kind. Here
are a few sentences from *To Whom the Goddess*:

> Few people will take on a gate in cold blood – few good
> hunters will jump even a small brook in cold blood – it
> is almost as if the Chase were a sort of dope. Possibly
> the artificial stimulation acts on glands in the body and
> gives super-vigour to both horse and rider. How else
> can one account for the stupendous leaps sometimes
> made out hunting over places that look impossible
> next day?

Not only is this a good example of my sister's style of writing, but
it also serves to illustrate the courage of the young eventers
nowadays who have to face their horses with 'stupendous leaps'
without the flow of adrenalin caused by the thrill of the chase,
with only the spur of competitive spirits driving them on.

The fact that Diana was able to illustrate her books as well as to write them is due in part to the encouragement and help she had from Lionel Edwards, a doctor's son from Chester, who often came to stay at Badminton. He was very much my father's protégé. My father gave him great encouragement when he was a young man for he needed not only persuasion but a certain amount of backing before deciding to dedicate himself to a life as a writer and artist.

The position of a governess in a large household such as ours at the turn of the century must have been a terribly difficult one, for, as the saying goes, she was neither fish, flesh nor good red herring. In no way could she be classed as one of us, nor was she exactly a servant. She had to hover in between like a tight-rope walker, and in almost as perilous a position, for it would be only too easy for her to make a slip and thus lose the respect of the servants. Equally she would have been given short shrift had she become too familiar with the grown-up members of the family. I do not imagine, for instance, that my father ever exchanged more than the briefest salutes with Miss Marshall, even though he had entrusted the all-important task of the education of his three children to her. My mother engaged her on the personal recommendation of a friend by whom she had been employed before she came to us.

That, in fact, is how nearly all the members of our staff used – and still do – to come to Badminton, either through recommendation or by relationship with someone already working for us. In those days they were never employed through an advertisement or from an employment agency. I don't think that my mother ever needed to have recourse to such measures, though naturally in the lower echelons, the Housekeeper and the Head Butler were responsible for both the hirings and the firings.

Life evidently did not change very much at Badminton during successive generations, for my grandfather's biographer gives an excellent description of life in the household in the 1870s:

> His household was a very splendid establishment, equalling in state and magnificence anything of the kind in the country. On a hunting morning the coach loaded with guests and friends, would be driven to the fixture by the Duke or Lord Worcester. [That would have been my father, of course.] When the day's sport

4. *With my father on the steps of the house before going out hunting one morning.*

5. *In my Coronation finery, 22 June 1911. I was train-bearer to my father who carried the Sword of Mercy in the great procession.*

was over, the Duke's guests would find a change of clothing and a lunch at some convenient inn, and could return in comfort to Badminton. From the first the Duke's children learned to ride.

We children of a generation later were no exception to that rule of early horsemanship. As soon as I could walk, I was put on to a donkey's back and taken to a nearby Meet of my father's hounds, though I cannot honestly say that I remember much about it. What I do remember, though, is admiring my sisters' neat turnouts in their Blue and Buff habits which were bestowed on them by their proud and indulgent father. Although they were not all that much older than me, they both took to the saddle quickly and easily, and they managed their smart little ponies extremely well, growing up, as I said before, to be superb and elegant horsewomen.

They had beautiful hands, and the bolder a horse, the more they liked it. Of course, they rode side-saddle, as it would have been unheard of for girls of their upbringing and background to have ridden astride in those days. I think it must have been the Great War that brought about a gradual change, as it was certainly in the 1920s that more and more women started to ride astride, and then they even began to compete against men in the show ring and on the point-to-point race-course.

In those Edwardian years before the Great War, as soon as we were let out of the schoolroom, we raced outside, oblivious of the weather, and as long as it was still light enough, we called together our motley pack of dogs and took them off to look for prey. My sisters were great huntsmen on foot, and between us we brought in a good many hares and rabbits which, if young enough, were eaten with relish by my parents, the older and tougher ones going to eke out many a cottage stock-pot.

However, there came a day when I was introduced to the gun by one of my father's keepers, Fred Young, and that day was destined to mark an epoch in my young life, for I took to shooting like the proverbial duck to water, which was much more than could truthfully be said about my riding. My lack of progress in the saddle must have been extremely puzzling to my father, and it must also have been a great disappointment. He always took great care to mount me on lovely little ponies of the sort of quality he believed suitable for his only son and heir. What he must have failed to realise was that I was in fact over-mounted, and all those quality ponies were far too strong for me, so naturally I was never really happy. It is no fun at all to be mounted on an animal that is pulling like a train and feels as if it is going to take off at any second and gallop without stopping until it eventually runs into an obstacle that is too big or wide for it to jump – especially if, like me when I was very young, you tend to be slightly nervous in the saddle.

What I think was perhaps my greatest drawback in my early riding career was the fact that I had been taught to ride and was always accompanied in the hunting field by my mother's old groom, Fred Matthews. He had come with my mother on her marriage from her previous home at Horton, and many years later, when I was grown-up, his son was to become my second horseman. Fred had had great success with my two sisters; unfortunately he tried the same methods with me which naturally proved disastrous, for he always shouted to me to lean back at the fences, having always been accustomed to instructing ladies. What of course he should have been doing was adjuring me to lean well forward. What happened? Naturally I fell off, not once but time after time, until I was not only absolutely fed up, but also in serious danger of losing my nerve.

Small wonder then that, on discovering my natural aptitude with a gun, I should infinitely prefer to accompany Fred Young where I could stand fairly and squarely on my own two feet potting at pigeons, crows and rabbits. A gun may have a kick, but I found that not nearly as painful as some of the tumbles I had hitherto taken from the backs of my ponies.

I soon discovered that I was not missed in the hunting field, so I used to slip away after an hour or two, leave my pony at the stables and then pick up my gun and join Fred Young. On looking back, I think it is quite probable that my father knew perfectly well what was happening, but chose to turn a blind eye. He was a very wise man, and knew me well, and he may have thought it better to leave me alone at that stage. However, I don't suppose he gave the matter a great deal of thought, for not only was he always very busy with his hunting, but also with all the other work that is involved in the running of a pack of hounds that in those days hunted six days a week. And not only did he have the hunting and the Estate to look after, but by sheer virtue of his position, a further multitude of duties fell to his lot. Having experienced all this myself for well over half a century, I know full well what calls there must have been on both his energy and on his time. I think he was really too busy to bother very much about me, and I dare say that like most of us when we are slightly worried about something, he pushed it to the back of his mind, optimistically hoping for the best and – as things eventually turned out – he was quite right to do so. He did, however, change his tactics a little in his purchase of ponies for me, and on my twelfth birthday, I received one called Woodcock that was to change my destiny.

As I spent day after day with Fred Young, so my shooting rapidly improved, and I raised my gun to my shoulder with greater and greater confidence. I was very fortunate to have such a good coach, for the lessons he taught me have stood me in good stead all my life, as nobody likes to disgrace themselves in a shooting line, me least of all.

When I was a young boy, we did not have an organised shoot at Badminton. The sporting life pivoted so much on fox-hunting that there was scarcely time to arrange anything else, let alone carry it out. When the grown-ups did go out with guns, they would walk up wild birds, and our keepers were not required to rear pheasants. Their duties were in fact much more concerned with covert-keeping and earth-stopping. In many ways, I think it was more fun like that, for there is certainly nothing I enjoy more than a few days on the grouse moors – nothing is wilder than a grouse – in the north of England where I used to go for a few days every year in August before we started cub-hunting, when my Godfather, Lord Lonsdale, known as the Yellow Earl, was still alive and living at Lowther Castle. Nowadays I still go north in August each year to stay with Anne, Duchess of Westminster, owner of the legendary Arkle, three-times winner of the Cheltenham Gold Cup and many other races. She has a house called Lochmore in Sutherland, and there I fish for salmon on the River Lexford and much enjoy the happy parties that gather there at that time of year. On my way up, I stop at Alnwick and stay with the Northumberlands not only to judge the young entry of their pack of foxhounds, the Percy, but also to have a couple of days' grouse-shooting. To my mind, reared birds, however high-flying, cannot be expected to produce quite the same sort of thrill or challenge as grouse. I find the beauty of the moors an additional bonus.

My ultimate change-over to what has proved to be a life-time's devotion to fox-hunting came about almost by accident. One spring day I came home from my private school for the Easter holidays by train, and when I finally reached Badminton, it was to find the new pony, Woodcock, all saddled up and waiting in the stables. All I had to do was to change quickly, mount him and go out to find hounds, for my train had arrived too late for me to attend the Meet.

As I trotted my pony smartly along a lane, I suddenly thought I heard something. Pulling up sharply – and for once I had an animal that was instantly obedient – I listened intently, hardly daring to breathe. The pony was evidently listening too and must have heard something, for his ears were pricked well forward, and he stood quite still like a little statue, though I could feel him trembling with excitement beneath me. This was catching, and I found my own excitement increasing with each successive moment. Sure enough, I found that my ears had not deceived me, for there was the unmistakable cry of hounds, and, what was more, though still in the distance, they were drawing closer every moment.

Now all my senses were alert and I stood and watched and listened for what seemed like hours, although probably only for a minute or two. Suddenly my patience was rewarded, for I caught sight of a big dog-fox slinking over a wall on the other side of the field right opposite where I stood. He paused for a moment, shooting a glance over his shoulder, and I could see that his tongue was lolling out. He did not come on towards me, but swiftly and quietly loped on across the end of that field, disappearing over a wall far over to my right.

Remembering everything I had been taught in the past, I glanced swiftly at my watch to note the time of the appearance of the fox, thankful that I had remembered to wind it up that morning, at the same time marking in my mind's eye the exact place where I had seen him disappear over that wall. Only a moment or two later, the leading hound came into sight over the fence at precisely the same spot where I had first caught sight of the fox. She too paused for an instant, but keeping her nose well to the ground, on she went, followed closely by the rest of the pack with a splendid cry.

To my utmost relief, the next figure to appear was that of the green-coated huntsman; as he came soaring over the wall, I stood up in my stirrups, holding out my cap in the direction the fox had gone. As the huntsman sped across the field in the direction I had indicated, following his hounds, I quickly popped over the wall directly in front of me – mercifully landing safely – and galloped across the field to join him.

George Walters, the huntsman, had not been long in our service, but he must quickly have realised that my heart was not genuinely in my hunting, and he evidently knew why, for as I came up behind him, he swiftly turned his head and shouted to me over his shoulder:

'Lean well forward as you come to the jumps, My Lord, and you'll be all right!'

That was just the sort of advice and encouragement I so sorely needed at the time, especially as I was riding a new pony, so I dug my heels into its sides and fell in behind the huntsman, remembering to keep a little to his side. Following his instructions, I did lean well forward as we approached each fence, my excitement growing as we cleared one after another. My gallant little pony, Woodcock, took them all in his stride, enjoying himself hugely, and there was I, still safely in the saddle.

Then followed one of the fastest and most exciting hunts I have ever had the good fortune to experience. For the first time in my life I found that I was really enjoying myself in the hunting field. Not only was my horsemanship improving minute by thrilling minute, but at last I was able to see for myself exactly what was happening. And not only that, but I also began to realise why my father and his friends were so interested in hounds and hound-work.

The pack were bunched together so tightly that you could have put the proverbial sheet over them, and as they sped along, still with that glorious cry, there was I, alone behind the huntsman and in the same field as hounds. To Sherston, then back to Luckington, across Badminton Park, and eventually just short of Hawkesbury Upton, the leading hound, that first beauty I had seen, bowled over the fox, the second one nipping it in the neck.

'Who-whoop! Who-whoop!' I shrieked as I pulled up my pony, and he stood there covered with sweat and with heaving sides, while the huntsman blew those ringing notes on his horn that announce to the world at large that hounds have successfully killed their fox in the open.

It was to be a long time before the rest of the Field gradually trickled in to the kill, for they had found themselves badly left in the Kilcot Hills. I must admit that this added to my triumph, for up to then it had always been me who was left, and never before had I been the only one in at a kill.

During the rest of those Easter holidays until the end of the hunting season I became more and more enthusiastic about the whole thing, and during the following summer months whenever I was at home, George Walters, the huntsman, set himself out to teach me all that he knew. He was a genuine, hardworking and kind man, a really knowledgeable foxhunter, and what he had to tell me I have remembered all my life. His advice and wisdom have been of the greatest value to me, and I owe him more than I can say, especially for that first piece of advice he gave me when he adjured me to lean well forward as I approached each jump.

And I must not forget that gallant pony, Woodcock. He was a topping little foxhunter, and he helped to build up the confidence that up to then I had so sadly lacked. That exciting and successful hunt I had so much enjoyed and concluded safely mounted on his back settled it – my destiny was assured. From that day on, I became a dedicated foxhunter, my gun lying abandoned, and for the time being, forgotten, on its rack.

> A southerly wind and a cloudy sky
>   Proclaim a hunting morning;
> Before the sun rises we nimbly fly,
>   Dull sleep and a drowsy bed scorning.
> To horse, my boys, to horse, away!
> The chase admits of no delay:
> On horseback we've got, together we'll trot,
> On horseback we've got, together we'll trot.
>   Leave off your chat, see the cover appear;
>   The hound that strikes first, cheer him without fear;
> Drag on him, ah! wind him, my steady good hounds!
> Drag on him, ah! wind him, the cover resounds!
>   (old hunting song)

CHAPTER 2

SCHOOLDAYS

My ninth birthday saw the end of petticoat government, for I was despatched to a private school called Wixenford, near Wokingham, in Berkshire. Wixenford was also not very many miles from the Garth Kennels at Mortimer, and as R. H. Gosling, an old friend of my father's, was the Master at that time, I have a strong suspicion that that was why the school was chosen for me. Then, if my father came to visit me, he could combine the two outings – seeing me, and also seeing the hounds. Now, sadly, the coming of the M4 motorway has made the country to the west of Wokingham unhuntable.

By the time I was nine, I had hardly been away from home, for my life had run on clearly defined lines. During the hunting season from the first of August, we lived at Badminton. On the first of May the house was shut up and we migrated, lock, stock and barrel, to Wales to stay at our house called Llangattock at Crickhowell, where we remained until the cub-hunting season started again. Although we would have visited Llangattock each year in any case, as it was our Welsh home, we were forced to abandon Badminton during the summer months owing to an acute shortage of water there.

For many years, the household had had to rely entirely on a pitifully inadequate supply of water from the pond in front of the house which is fed from land water and replenished by rainfall – totally inadequate in those days because there was such a great call on its resources. Up to 1899, when my father succeeded, every drop of water that was used in the house had to be carried. He then had pipes laid from the reservoir at Luckley Brake to the house. Recently I had those pipes dug up, and they were found to be in as good order as they were the day they were laid eighty years before.

As you can imagine, the consumption of water in a house the size of Badminton, especially when it was full of guests, was enormous. Nearly everybody who came to stay with us – and there were a good many – indulged in fairly strenuous forms of exercise, and therefore they all needed daily immersion. This meant that water had to be carried up to their bedrooms to fill the hip-baths that were kept in cupboards and carried out to be placed in front of open fires with strategically positioned screens around them. Quite apart from that sort of domestic consumption, even more water was needed to keep the house and garden in good trim, to say nothing of the massive daily requirements of the stables and those of the kennels.

A more delicate matter, which was dealt with by the Clerk of the Works – quite an appropriate name I think! – was the provision of suitable sanitary arrangements. In the case of the ladies, this consisted of commodes which were either in the bedrooms themselves or in closets just off the rooms. The gentlemen were obliged to retire a couple of hundred yards to an outside latrine that had been dug on the same lines as those used by soldiers in army camps, completely hidden by a suitable screen of dense bushes. Although well away from the house on the east side, an easterly wind could prove a trifle malodorous.

At the time of droughts, the poor Clerk of the Works must have torn his hair, for the Park Pond was scarcely adequate at the best of times, and I imagine he had to study its level very carefully, and that his prayers each night began with the ones containing the words:

> ... Send us, we beseech Thee, in this our necessity,
> such moderate rain and showers, that we may receive
> the fruits of the earth to our comfort.

Eventually, not long before the Great War, the whole difficult situation was resolved by one of our neighbours who lived at a house then called Weston Birt – now known as Westonbirt, a school for girls. He was Sir George Holford, an amateur geologist of some distinction and a superb forester like his father before him, who in about 1869 had started the famous Arboretum where every known tree that can be grown in this country is now to be found.

Sir George, who had been in the Life Guards and was an extra Equerry to King George V, was absolutely convinced from the way in which his trees grew that great underground reservoirs of water existed under the land in the vicinity of his house – and he owned sixteen thousand acres of land. But nothing he could do or say seemed to persuade the local authorities to go along and carry out the quite simple tests that would prove whether or not there was any truth in his theory. However, luckily for us at Badminton, a newcomer who was evidently more enlightened, appeared on the Council. The long overdue tests were carried out, and Sir George was proved right. The West Gloucestershire Water Company was formed. Exactly as Sir George had always predicted and right under his own land, they found great and hitherto untapped natural reservoirs of water. These stretched right away under the ground that lies between Shipton Moyne and Westonbirt. Now this water has been piped into and through a central reservoir at Tolldown just off the Bath–Stroud junction of the M4, and serves the Vale of Sodbury and parts of Bath. The water for Badminton and the surrounding villages comes from a similar reservoir at Luckley Brake, which, although the actual reservoir had been there for years, had always been pitifully inadequate. This was now replenished through extra supplies of water coming by pipes laid from Westonbirt, and that water is piped on from Luckley Brake to Badminton House via the Mount Pond.

For old times' sake, I have retained a clause in my tenancy agreements requiring tenants of all my cottages and farmhouses to keep their dewponds dug out each year. A more important clause appears in the bye-laws of the Westonbirt Arboretum, and this has been there since the very beginning: while prohibiting ridden horses to go through those grounds, it clearly states that an exception would always be made for those ridden by members of the staff of the Duke of Beaufort and his successors.

So apart from those annual visits to Wales, and an occasional trip to London to visit the doctor and the dentist, I scarcely ever left Badminton during my early childhood. There were two or three holidays at the seaside when one of us children had been ill or under the weather.

One of those visits took place in 1907 when both my mother and I had our appendixes out, being operated on by Sir Alfred Fripp, the surgeon who had previously performed the same operation on King Edward VII. Although my mother decided to convalesce at home, I was sent down to Woolacombe on the North Devon coast with my sisters, accompanied by Sarah Meadows, our nurse. In those days Woolacombe was a tiny and relatively unknown seaside village with a vast stretch of sandy beach that runs for two or three miles as far as Putsborough. The great Atlantic breakers come crashing in spectacularly; nowadays that beach is much in demand for surf riders, who bring their boards from all over the country. Although I remember it as being a very windy place, my sisters and I did not surf ride but used to enjoy far less sophisticated pleasures, looking for shells and little fish in the rocky pools that lie under the northern cliff face. We would, like all other children who have a seaside holiday, build giant moated sandcastles; then wait eagerly for the tide to come in, and watch the swirling water first fill our moat, going on to destroy the whole of our afternoon's work. We would philosophically turn our faces towards the house where we were staying, knowing that we could build just such another the following day.

If I had an infectious disease at home, I was packed off forthwith to stay with the butler, David Head, at his cottage that lies at the gates to Badminton House, where his daughter, Winnie, who later married Lord Suffolk's butler and went to live at Charlton Park near Malmesbury, looked after me so well that when I was better I didn't want to go back home. I fancy that she really spoilt me, letting me do just what I pleased, and I suspect that my nurse had quite a time getting me back into the normal nursery routine again after one of those visits. Of course, people were much more scared of infection then, which was understandable in those days before the discovery and widespread use of antibiotics, for what started out by being only a simple case of measles only too frequently produced complications which, in turn, led to a severe and serious case of pneumonia which often proved fatal, especially in small children.

Although in the last century there were many reforms brought in to protect young children from abuse when they were employed in coal mines and factories, nobody thought about the poor unfortunates who were often the innocent victims of the strength of a school-master's arm, driven on by his unjustified anger, and my own grandfather was such a one. When he was at his private school at Brighton he committed what appeared to be the unforgivable crime of ending a pentameter with a three-syllable word, and was immediately punished for this offence by the usher in charge of the class. Still not content, the Headmaster summoned the poor little boy to his study and beat him again, sending him away with the promise of more to come the next morning. It was a bitterly cold day in November, and my grandfather woke at daybreak; and then with no overcoat, only one glove and a groat – a fourpenny piece – he crept under the front gate and made haste for the stableyard from which he knew his father's coach, the 'Wonder' would shortly be starting for London. This was a stage-coach that my great-grandfather kept on the road himself, and the boy reached it to find the horses being put to. With a certain amount of cunning he spun the coachman, Capps, a yarn telling him that he wanted to go to London to visit his father who was ill with gout. However, his guile did not extend to giving him enough sense to hide away inside the coach; instead, he sat on the box with the coachman – thus in the following hue and cry, news came back to the school that the coach had gone with a young boy sitting on the box. It happened that the Headmaster's son was at home from Cambridge, and he took his father's best horse, Vagabond, and pursued that coach, catching up with it at Horley. By this time, the astute coachman had put two and two together and had seen to it that the boy was inside the coach. However, the Headmaster's undergraduate son, showing no signs that his own youth gave him any pity for another boy and probably driven on by the knowledge of the disgrace that would follow for his father should it become known that so important a pupil had run away from the school, and the reason why – dragged the unfortunate boy out of the coach while the horses were being changed. Together they returned in a post-chaise, with Vagabond tied to the hand-horse. Poor Vagabond was nearly done, and my grandfather was more concerned about the condition of that horse than he was about the retribution that he would meet on his return to that hated school. Sure enough, the Headmaster vent the full force of his ire on the boy, birching the child until he could no longer lift his arm to administer the strokes – and, sad to say, poor Vagabond was never to recover from that forced gallop. Nor did my great-grandparents take their son away from the school.

With this story in mind, it was obviously with mixed feelings that I left Badminton for my first term at boarding school. On the one hand I was rather looking forward to it, even if the other half of me was very apprehensive, for I was eager to play team games with other boys, as up to then I had not known very many boys of my own age, apart from the sons of estate workers. However, I need not have had any worries, for I took to my new life quickly and readily, within a week or two feeling as if I had always been at the school. I was helped I dare say by the fact that my father had had a professional cricket coach down to teach me and the village boys the elements of the game. Although this seemed to be a very generous gesture on his part, it also paid a handsome dividend, for the Badminton cricket eleven was to beat all comers, as the members of our village team had all been so well grounded in the arts of that fine game.

Looking back, I realise now that I had led a very sheltered life up to then, for I had never really had to stand up for myself. I had not even handled money, except for my Church collection, and that was always put in my hand by my mother just before the bag came round. When I wanted to buy some sweets, all I had to do was to go to the local shop, Drewett's, choose something and take it away, no cash changing hands. My packets of liquorice, toffees or gob-stoppers were just put down on our general household accounts.

In spite of the fact that my home had been the absolute centre and hub of my whole existence for my first nine years, I genuinely do not remember feeling in the least homesick when I went off to school. The rough and tumble of school life thoroughly suited me, and to tell you the truth, I think I was quite relieved to find myself in an all-male establishment at last. It must be remembered that I only had sisters close to me in age, as my half-brothers, Freddy and Maurice de Tuyll, were too old to take much notice of a small boy like me. I dare say they found things a little difficult, as obviously there was a great fuss made of me as my father's only son and heir. On the other hand, I know that both my parents went out of their way to be scrupulously fair to the five of us.

As I settled down at school so quickly and happily, I found that I made friends very easily and more than held my own in the mob of small boys. Naturally, it was all quite different from home, but I simply loved the games and quickly became a most enthusiastic and quite proficient cricketer. This has been an interest that has lasted all my life. Little did I think as I stood at the wicket at Wixenford during that summer of 1909, with my pads nearly as big as me, that some forty years later I would be asked to be President of the MCC in Coronation year, when we regained the Ashes, and the Queen attended the final Test Match. Nor that I would invite such giants as Wally Hammond and Tom Goddard to come and play cricket at Badminton, though in doing this I was carrying on a well-honoured family tradition, as my father had always encouraged first-class cricket on the lawn in front of the house.

I fear that lessons did not make much of an impact on me, for I can remember very little about them, though mathematics, Latin, geography and history were added to my previous curriculum which up to then had been limited in the main to the three Rs. I am afraid I always felt that what went on in the classroom was a tiresome necessity breaking into the more important and never-failing joys of the playing fields.

I imagine that private schools for boys – or preparatory schools as they are more often called nowadays, except by Etonians who stick to the same old name – have not changed much with the years; I expect they were more comfortable in my time though, for in those days it was so much easier to get domestic staff, and therefore the catering side was bound to be better. We all slept in big dormitories with a senior boy in charge, whose duty it was to supervise us and see to it that we did not get up to mischief after lights out when we were supposed to settle down and go to sleep. However, the days were arranged with sufficient outdoor exercise to ensure that we were asleep almost as soon as our heads touched the pillows, only to wake up with a start to the clanging of the getting-up bell the next morning.

I can remember the excitement among the boys from hunting families like me when the Garth Hunt was meeting locally, for we always hoped against hope that they would run near the school. How we loved it if they did. Down would go our books, our pens, our pencils, and out we would rush to cheer them on, completely oblivious of calls from the masters, though I imagine they themselves were nearly as pleased as we were to have a break in their routine.

In those days it was not the fashion for parents to visit their children at school, and very often the appearance of a mother meant that something was seriously wrong at home. Our only contact with our families was by the medium of letters, for the telephone in my youth was only used for long-distance, or trunk calls as they were called then, in cases of dire emergency; it took so long to get through, that often it was quicker to send a telegram. We were made to write home every Sunday afternoon; then on Wednesday mornings, as regularly as clockwork I would find a nice long letter from my mother in my pigeonhole. She used to write and tell me everything that was happening at Badminton, and one of my regrets is that I did not keep any of her letters. I rarely had a letter from my father though, but I knew it was not from lack of affection, but genuinely through lack of time – he relied on his wife to keep me in touch. He made up for the lack of communication in the term by giving me as much attention as he could during the holidays.

Our lives at Wixenford were regulated by a strict timetable; we rose at about seven o'clock in the summer, half an hour later in the winter, washed in cold water, a trifle sketchily I fear, and then raced downstairs to devour a substantial breakfast. The food was excellent; many schools in those days were proud of the fact that they ran their own farms from which they drew all their dairy produce, and ours certainly produced home-grown vegetables. Most of the boys at Wixenford came from the same sort of sporting homes as mine – though perhaps not so large – and we were all accustomed to what many people nowadays would consider to be fairly spartan conditions, for few houses were centrally heated, and schools were no exception to that general rule. We were expected to, and we did, keep ourselves warm and the blood circulating in our veins by means of hard physical exercise. I think that those early days at school and my hunting in the holidays helped me to build up a sound constitution that has never failed me, except when my diet has been wrong, which happened during the last war when I developed acute gastric ulcers.

After we had gulped down our portions of bacon and sausages or whatever else was on the table for breakfast that morning, and devoured as many pieces of bread and butter and marmalade as time would permit, the bell rang for prayers. These were held in the School Chapel, a big room off the ground floor, and those poor unfortunates who took lessons on the piano had to take it in turns to accompany us as we lustily sang the hymns.

I had had lessons on the piano with Miss Marshall, and these were continued at Wixenford, but when I went to Eton my piano lessons and practice would have had to come out of my free time, and I thought that would take too large a bite from the hours I wanted to devote entirely to games. I much regret it now though, for I would love to be able to accompany the sing-songs we enjoy so much at Badminton. I love singing in the right surroundings and conditions, but I did everything in my power to avoid being put in the choir at Wixenford. I was very careful to sing out of tune when I was taking the obligatory test – and the same applied when I went on to Eton. I had no wish to dress up every Sunday and be obliged to attend services twice a day.

I did not find the lessons that followed prayers very exciting, but that was through no fault of the teachers, for I am sure they were first-class. There was the new and added incentive of competition with my peers, and the subjects were a good deal more varied and comprehensive than those I had had up to then with my sisters' governess. But all the same, I suppose the fact is that I was never particularly eager to learn, for I always found that towards the end of each morning when the enticing smells started to drift into our classroom from the kitchens, my mind would wander off and I would begin to contemplate the prospect of the games that would follow luncheon after we had had a short rest.

Our school terms were not divided in any way as they are today, and we had no free or exeat weekends, not even a half-term holiday. We rarely left the school premises unless we were in a school team and then we would go off on an occasional afternoon to play an away match against another school. That was fun, because we were able to compare their conditions with our own, and there was always a lovely tea laid on after the match, for each school was anxious to out-rival the others with the hospitality they offered. I was amused to meet an ex-Master of Hounds, Jack Moore-Stevens, during one of my eightieth birthday celebrations, and to hear that when he had been at a rival private school, he had been beaten by his Headmaster because he had kicked me on the shins during one of those long-ago matches!

We were sometimes permitted to go out to Sunday luncheon after Chapel with a visiting Godparent, uncle or aunt, if sufficient notice had been given. I was always glad if my Godfather, Lord Lonsdale, came, for he always pressed a lovely crackling five-pound note into my hand as he left – and that large piece of white paper really meant something in those days. At the end of term, I returned home on my own by rail, my trunk having gone on in advance; I was met at the station by the under coachman with whatever conveyance happened to be free at the time.

When the Great Western Railway Company first broached the subject of a proposed railway line crossing my father's property, he considered the idea for a long time. Finally he agreed to the proposition, saying that he would make no charge for the land involved, provided that when he, members of his family and guests wished to travel by rail, they would have the right to stop trains at a local station. In order to bring the railway across the estate, it was necessary to excavate a long railway tunnel to come out in the Sodbury Vale; as such tunnels need ventilation, the resulting airshafts, castellated like mini-fortresses, have always given rise to a certain amount of speculation. I know that there are two schools of untutored thought, one of them seriously believing that the towers are some form of ancient fortifications, and the other believing, just as seriously, that they are follies which were built by my ancestors. The more prosaic truth does not seem to occur to them. When British Rail came into existence after the last war their Chairman, Dr Beeching (now a life peer) closed down the majority of country stations, and by this action we were stripped of our privileges for Badminton was one of the victims – but we had no compensation for the land over which the railway runs, even though if we now want to travel by rail, we have to go as far afield as Bristol, Chippenham or Swindon, as people did in the early days of the railways back in the reign of Queen Victoria. Such is progress!

After we broke up, from the moment I set foot on the platform of Badminton station, all thoughts of school went right out of my mind, and I looked forward eagerly to the joy of the sight of my beloved home and the coming reunion with my parents, my sisters and my animals. If it was the end of the winter term I became excited at the prospect of the forthcoming Christmas festivities when the house was always filled with my parents' friends and their children, and we were invited to party after party throughout the holidays. Christmas Day, of course, was itself full of excitement, starting with the stocking that 'Father Christmas', alias my mother, never forgot. After breakfast and before Church we opened our presents, which were piled in heaps under the Christmas tree in the drawing-room, labelled with the name of each child. Like all children, we tore open the parcels with feverish fingers.

Our upbringing was not, thank goodness, nearly as rarified as that of some of my ancestors, judging by an early account:

> ... The children of the family were bred with a philosophical care. No inferior servants were permitted to entertain them, lest some mean sentiments or foolish notions and fables should steal into them, and nothing was so strongly impressed upon them as a sense of honour. Witness the Lord Arthur, who, being about five years old, was very angry with the judge for hanging men. The judge told him that if they were

6. *During my first Half at Eton when I was too small to wear tails.*

7. *Tom Newman with a stallion hound.*

8. *The stuffed wolf in the Steward's Room – my grand-father's French trophy.*

not hanged they would kill and steal. 'No,' said the little boy, 'you should make them promise upon their honour they will not do so, and then they will not!'

Even if we three were not brought up with quite such high standards of care and behaviour, I doubt very much whether my mother would have been very pleased had she known of certain visits we made to the stables.

At about the time of my birth, a man called Tom Newman came into my father's hunt service, and he later became huntsman, hunting hounds for fifteen seasons, in spite of the fact that he was turned down by the army in 1914 as being unfit for active service! When the news came to us that Tom had come home from his annual holiday, we used to race down to the stables and listen spellbound to his stories. For Tom's best friend was a policeman in the London CID, and Tom always spent his holidays with him, accompanying him when he went into the seedy corners of Soho and the East End. Tom would then return to Badminton with a fund of hair-raising yarns and anecdotes, ranging from tales of forgery and pick-pocketing to the far worse crimes of murder and arson. Naturally we kept these sessions a great secret from our mother, for we did not want to be stopped from missing a word; however enthralling were his stories, I am sure Tom Newman never overstepped the mark, and kept the really gory details to himself.

One day we ourselves had an excitement that capped the best of Tom's yarns. When motor cars first began to be used by all and sundry, my father, always ready to move with the times, bought his first one, a Panhard. In those early days of motoring it was the fashion to employ a French chauffeur, so my father engaged a man with impeccable references. Just after Christmas that year, my sisters and I and a couple of other children who had been staying with us were taken to the pantomime at the Theatre Royal in Bristol by Miss Marshall. We had been looking forward to this outing for days, so it was with great excitement that we stepped into the Panhard, the smart liveried chauffeur holding open the door for us.

When we arrived at the theatre, we were met by the Manager, who himself led us to our box on the right hand side of the stage, and we had a lovely view. How we enjoyed the entertainment, the songs and the dancing and the colourful costumes. From our box we could not only watch what was happening on the stage, but we could also see the orchestra and wonder at the nimble fingers of the pianist as they went up and down the keyboard.

During the interval when we were all eating ice-creams – another rare treat – the Manager came to our box again to tell Miss Marshall that a message had been received to the effect that the Panhard had broken down, so the French chauffeur had arranged for a hired car to come to the theatre at the end of the performance to take us home. In those days, there was nothing unusual about such a message. Cars were always either breaking down or having punctures, so when the pantomime had ended, the cast had taken their final curtain call, applauded enthusiastically by us children, and the last strains of the National Anthem had died away, without question we piled into the big hired car that, sure enough, we found waiting for us outside – there were no double yellow lines in those days!

We did not give the Panhard or the chauffeur another thought; but late the following day we were told that our so-called French 'chauffeur' was nothing of the sort, being none other than an internationally notorious jewel thief for whom the police had been looking for a long time. The evening of the pantomime, after dropping us at the Theatre Royal in Bristol, he had then driven my father's Panhard hell for leather to London. Once there, he carried out a daring burglary and set off in the Panhard once more for the coast at Dover. Abandoning the car by the dockside, he had boarded a boat that would carry him back to his native country.

However, all did not go to plan, for when he stepped off the train at Paris, he found himself surrounded by policemen, and it was only a matter of minutes before he was travelling back again to London, handcuffed to an English detective-inspector from the Metropolitan Police Force. At Victoria he was charged with several of his earlier crimes, as well as the most recent one.

You can imagine the excitement this caused in the nursery at Badminton. We rushed down to the stables to get in first with the news to Tom Newman, and could talk of nothing else for days.

I think that, although we naturally had a careful upbringing, we were given a lot more freedom than most children in our position, as we lived downstairs and were not restricted to the nursery. We mixed with our parents' guests, which was a very good thing, for it saved us from the shyness that besets many

young people in their teens, and we found ourselves able to hold
our own in conversations with grown-ups.

I had always taken it for granted that I would go to Eton when I
was thirteen after leaving my private school, though I am told
that it was not very usual, even then, for ducal families to send
their sons to school. So my father was rather a pioneer; but he
was in good company, for King George V sent his third son,
Henry, Duke of Gloucester, to Eton on the same day as me, and
his name appears in the School Register as 'HRH Prince Henry –
Buckingham Palace'. The sons of most Dukes – and, after all,
apart from the Royal ones, there are only twenty-seven of us, of
which my own Dukedom ranks fifth in order of precedence –
were mostly educated privately by tutors at home, and in earlier
days were often sent on a Grand Tour of Europe to complete
their education. I am sure that those tours must have done a
great deal, both to widen their horizons and also to provide them
with a foundation and background of knowledge, so that on
their return, they found themselves better able to understand
and appreciate to the full all the beautiful things in their own
homes. Many of them, of course, brought back new treasures to
add to their family collections, and the 3rd and 4th Dukes of
Beaufort, about whom I shall be talking later, were no exception.
    Going abroad has never held much appeal for me, as all my
interests have always centred in this country, but when I was
very young, my mother used to take me with her when she went
with her other two sons, Freddy and Maurice de Tuyll, to visit
their numerous Dutch relations who still lived in Holland, and I
enjoyed those trips.
    When I went to Eton, although we had to sit an examination to
determine what place we would take in the school, we were not
required to pass a Common Entrance exam, which I am told is
the bugbear of small boys – and their parents – today. It says a lot
for the teaching of both Miss Marshall and the masters at Wixenford that, much to my surprise, I went straight into Remove, for I
cannot say that I had ever been what you might call a rewarding
pupil. All that was required then to enter Eton was a basic
standard of education, and a reasonable assumption that our
parents could afford to pay the fees. In those days I imagine that
there was also slightly more emphasis on social standing. As
both my parents were anxious for me to follow in my father's
footsteps and go into the Blues when I left school, I was entered
for what was then known at Eton as the Army Class, into which

boys destined for Army careers went when they were about sixteen. One of the great advantages of this course to me was the fact that our classical education was confined to a mere five or six hours of Latin each week, which was still more than enough to my mind.

I was up to John Christie for mathematics and science. He was a most colourful character, famous for having founded and built the famous opera at Glyndebourne for his wife, who was a very talented singer. Before John Christie was permitted to inherit the family fortune that lay in estates in North Devon, he was required to prove that he could hold down a regular job, and this he certainly did at Eton, teaching with flair and all-round entertainment for his pupils for sixteen years.

Of course, I knew a good many boys who were already at Eton, and several contemporaries from my private school started on the same day at the beginning of the Michaelmas Half, as it is known at Eton, 1913. Terms are always called Halves at Eton, as in 1440 when the school was founded by Henry VI, himself then only twenty years old, academic years were divided into only two parts; the custom of using the word 'Half' has been maintained ever since.

Even so, the very idea of going to such a large school with nearly five hundred years of tradition and more than a thousand pupils was quite intimidating. I had a rough idea of what to expect from things I had been told by my friends at home who were already at Eton, and I knew that it was unlikely that I would be 'kippered' over an open fire like the poor hero of *Tom Brown's Schooldays*, nor was I likely to suffer the fate of my grandfather who was so badly beaten at Brighton. My own father had a pasting at Eton when he arrived back late one Half in 1863, when he was sixteen. He returned with what he considered a perfectly good excuse. My grandfather was invited to take some of his hounds to France on a wolf-hunting expedition, an invitation that followed an enquiry from the Master of a wolf-hunting pack in Poitou who had approached my grandfather with a request that he might be allowed to buy some of the Beaufort hounds. We never sell our hounds, but my grandfather sent him several couple, and later embarked from Folkestone for a visit to France.

The party must have presented a remarkable sight as they boarded the cross-Channel ferry. There were twenty-five couple of hounds – this being before the time of the quarantine laws, which only came into being in 1902 after all the rabies scares of the last century – eighteen horses, two carriages and a baggage cart. My grandfather's arrival in France was described in the French *Journal de la Vienne*, a sort of Gallic *Horse and Hound*, thus:

> The Duke of Beaufort has just passed through Paris with two hundred dogs intended to destroy the wolves which are here the terror of the shepherd and of the inhabitants of lonely dwellings. It may be said of the peer that he is a sportsman by profession. He has inherited a rental of a million francs on condition that he shall always maintain three packs of hounds, and shall hunt six days a week. Another clause in the will binds him to expend 250,000 francs a year on his hunting establishment. There are collaterals always on the watch who would cause the bequest to be revoked in case the conditions are not carried out. These noble eccentricities are to be found only in England.

My grandfather had some doubts about the ability of his hounds to hunt wolves successfully, entered as they were to fox and to fox alone; but he need not have worried, for as soon as they saw the French hounds killing their prey, they took readily to the scent of wolf. It was reported that he brought back one carcase, had it stuffed and mounted and put in a glass case in the dining-room. It was in fact put in the Steward's Room, which we used as a dining-room for some time when the rest of the house was out of action, and there it remains to this day.

However much my father had enjoyed this new experience, he suffered when he returned to Eton, for his excuse was not accepted by the powers-that-be, and he was swiped for what was really an offence committed by his father. There seems to be no justice among school-masters: at any rate, not among those of the last century, for I must admit that I myself never had any reason to complain.

When I first went to Eton, I found that, after spending four years or so at Wixenford, where everything that happened was predictable and we always knew what to do next, Eton seemed a huge and exciting world, though I was a little over-awed for a few days. The greatest change of all was the fact that I now had my own room, where I found I was expected to do most of my out-of-school work without supervision. This was my own domain, and it offered me a certain degree of privacy.

I can well remember my first day at Eton. My mother took me

there, and she went prepared; after all, she had two older sons, and therefore knew the ropes. We were shown up to the room that I would occupy for that year. It was very small and rather bare, but in a jiffy my mother had pulled out a small hammer and some tacks from a bag that she was carrying and, before you could say 'knife', she had hopped on to a chair and was starting to hang several pictures she had had sent on with the rest of my luggage, which, as well as my clothes, included curtains and a small armchair. Suddenly the door burst open, and in came a scandalised Dame, who, caring not a jot that the culprit was a Duchess, proceeded in terse and acid terms to lay down exactly just what was permitted and what was most definitely *not* permitted in a boy's room – it seemed that the worst offence of all was to drive nails into those sacred walls.

The Dame is a lady who looks after the domestic side of a Boys' House as far as its inmates are concerned. She acts as a sort of bridge between the austerity of school life and the comforts of home, and often becomes a personal friend of many of the parents and also of the boy himself; she can play a very important part in the life of a boy at Eton. It is the Dame who orders food for the boys, engages the domestic staff and sees to it that the house runs smoothly and efficiently, organising the laundry, cleaning and all the hundred and one things that have to be done in a large household. As well as being a superior kind of housekeeper, she also acts more or less *in loco parentis*, keeping an eye on the health and general well-being of her charges. If she has managed to establish a good relationship with the boys under her care, she will be rewarded by both their affection and their loyalty.

As boys go up the school at Eton, so they progressively become entitled to a bigger and better room that is lower and lower down the building; so beginning with a small room at the back of the top floor, by the end of his fourth year, a boy will probably have graduated to a larger one at the front of the first floor. It may seem strange to an outsider that at a school of Eton's standing and fame, the boys should be expected to provide their own furniture, but in a way it does help to bring a little home atmosphere back to school.

In my day a system was followed whereby each House Master ran his own House as a separate entity, submitting his own accounts to the parents for board and lodgings. The Eton College Bursar was responsible only for the collection of tuition fees. It was generally said that Eton House Masters needed to make enough money during the fifteen or so years they had a House to enable them to provide for their old age, and I dare say that in some isolated cases there may have been some abuse of this system – in other words, money that should have been spent on food and comforts for the boys going straight into the House Master's own pocket. Certainly when I was there, some houses were notorious for their spartan conditions, but I was very fortunate in having as my House Master R. S. Kindersley, for the boys in his care had excellent food and living conditions. The House itself was called The Timbralls, and it stands right next to the field where the famous Eton Field Game is played. This field has three names, being known as Sixpenny in the Summer Half, the Field in the Michaelmas Half, and the Timbralls at all other times. Houses are never known by their own names to the boys, but by their House Master's initials when they refer to it in school, and by his surname when they talk to people outside. So if I was asked by someone during the holidays whose House I was in, my answer would be 'R. S. Kindersley's'.

Before Richard Kindersley had that House, he was in charge of what was called a 'holding house' where boys go to wait for a place to become free in their permanent one. This House was called Baldwins End, and one night a terrible fire broke out. On hearing some boys who were trapped on the top floor calling for help Richard Kindersley courageously climbed right up the out-side of the House in what was, alas, a vain attempt to save them. There were bars on the windows, and so he was obliged to go down again and leave them to their tragic fate. That experience had the most profound effect on him, and I was told that from being a cheery sort of person, he changed character; certainly when I knew him, he had a most sad expression, and, needless to say, he was almost fanatical about the fires in our rooms, coming round each night without fail to make absolutely certain for himself that every ember had died.

When the wife of an old-Etonian is expecting her first child, the couple make enquiries among their friends and find out the names of Assistant Masters at Eton who are preparing 'lists'. These are the Masters who will eventually get a House; but that will not be for several years, so in the meantime they collect the names of boys to whom they will eventually be able to offer places. It is entirely up to the individual Master whether or not he offers any particular boy a vacancy in his House, so the system tends to be a personally selective one, as obviously a man is going to fill his House with the sort of boys he thinks will fit in well with the general atmosphere and activities. If the future House Master, for instance, favours rowing, then naturally he will be more likely to take the sons of men who have been successful oars themselves, and of course this rule of thumb applies equally to cricketers.

The wife of a House Master plays an important part in the smooth running of her husband's House, for it is her responsibility to do all the entertaining that is necessary for her husband on the private side of the House. During a boy's time at Eton, his parents are invited fairly regularly to have a meal or a drink with the House Master, and so the close relationship that can develop between a boy and his House Master becomes extended to his whole family. The good Masters tend to take the view that what happens to the family is also their concern, as it is bound to have an effect on a boy in their care.

When I arrived at Eton, I must have been under 5 ft 4 in tall, for I had to wear an abominable Eton suit with a big stiff and desperately uncomfortable collar. Mercifully I grew very fast, and soon graduated to what is called 'School dress' which consists of a black tailcoat with striped trousers, a white shirt with a stiff collar and a small white tie.

In fact I grew very fast – much too fast – for as I shot up, I found that I had more and more trouble with my eyes. Eventually it was discovered that I was short-sighted, and so glasses were prescribed, and these I have had to wear throughout the whole of my life for distance. This disability has been a real affliction to me throughout my hunting life, as spectacles are a terrible drawback for that particular sport. When they are not misted over with heat, then they are wet with rain; it is no fun at all having to hunt hounds when you can scarcely see as far as the next fence, and ten to one, you will have to jump it blind. I did try contact lenses before the war when they had just been invented, but I found that I could only keep them in for an hour or two at a time. People today do not know how lucky they are to be able to have the tiny plastic lenses that have taken the place of those clumsy pieces of glass I had to learn to insert in my eyes and which made them so sore and runny.

Eton is, of course, a school that thrives on tradition, and as a boy progresses up the school, so his status gradually changes and improves. I began as a small boy at the beck and call of his fagmasters – and I had to do my fair share of that, my fagmaster being Chatty Hilton-Green, then Master of the Eton Beagles, the son of a great friend and neighbour of ours, and later one of the best amateur huntsmen of his time, especially when he was Master of the Cottesmore and hunted hounds himself. I expect it was all very good for me, as fagging is supposed to be the means whereby older and more responsible boys take some share in the training of their juniors. While the younger boy learns to take orders and carry them out cheerfully and with a good heart, the older one not only learns to give those orders, but also has practical lessons in self-restraint and tact, both of them qualities likely to be of use to him in after life. I had to be on call at certain times of the day so that I could leap into action when my fagmaster wanted some toast made, some coal brought upstairs, or a message fetched or carried.

I found that in common with other boys who were my contemporaries (some of their names come to mind: Hugh Kindersley who eventually became President of the Eton Society, R. J. G. Boothby, who messed with me – which means that we had tea together in one of our rooms – and later became Lord Boothby of television fame, and Ralph Roper-Curzon, Lord Teynham's son, who eventually went into the Scots Guards after serving as an oil engineer during the last few months of the Great War) I became more and more privileged as the years sped by.

When I was going on for seventeen, I was elected into what is known as Pop, or the Eton Society, which is a very exclusive band of boys. It is a self-electing body which has its own club-room where occasional debates are held and where the election of new members takes place. It enjoys very great prestige in the eyes of the other boys, and membership carries the privileges of being able to wear a waistcoat of the fanciest hue and material, a stick-up-collar and also to sport a flower in the buttonhole. In addition, members of Pop have their tail coats braided round the edges and they are permitted to wear 'sponge-bag' trousers, ones that are made of black and white checked material instead of the otherwise obligatory stripes. Those distinctions were otherwise only allowed to the Sixth Form in my day, though I am told that they are now extended to people like House Captains, Games Captains (or Keepers as they are more often known at Eton) and winners of University Scholarships.

The tail coats that are traditionally worn by Etonians are a form of mourning for King George III, the famous annual jamboree that takes place on the Fourth of June being in celebration of his birthday. That much maligned king was a great benefactor to Eton, and his memory lives on there. So it was on the anniversary of the birth of George III, in 1914 that I attended my only peacetime Fourth of June which came at the end of my first year at Eton. It is the only one that I remember, for in subsequent years, my mother whipped me off to London to visit friends. My father was unable to come to that last peacetime party, so my mother came alone. After lunch which we had in my House, we strolled through the school playing-fields on our way to watch the cricket. My mother met a great many of her friends, and stood about talking with them in the summer sunshine. I well remember that all the ladies wore beautiful clothes with enormous hats, and they nearly all carried parasols. My mother was no exception, and I was very proud of her, for she was dressed in a lovely pale blue silk outfit that had been made for her in London. Blue was always her favourite colour, and in my mind's eye I always remember her in one or other shade of blue. Another of my earliest memories is that of the fragrance of her scent which I adored, and if I were to smell a whiff of it now, even today, which is thirty-five years after her death on the eve of what would have been her fiftieth wedding anniversary, such would be my nostalgia that I would be certain that either she was about to appear, or that she had just left the room. The scent came to her regularly from Floris, the world-famous *parfumier* who is still to be found in Jermyn Street. My mother went to London for her riding habits and for all the clothes that she wanted for special occasions, her everyday clothes being made by a local dressmaker. This local woman also made my sisters' frocks – though my mother took them with her to London for their habits.

It seemed strange on that summer day in June so long ago to see all those fashionable ladies and gentlemen parading up and down our school playing-fields that were normally filled with hordes of muddy boys rushing about on their way from one game or another.

In the afternoon there was a splendid parade of boats, and everybody crowded down to the riverbank at Fellows Eyot in time to get a good view of the fleet of ancient rowing boats that came gliding into sight, and one after the other they approached the expectant crowds. As the first boat drew parallel to the spectators, on the piping command of their diminutive cox attired in full admiral's uniform of the time of George III complete with sword, which he drew just before he shouted his command, one by one the members of the crew stood their oars up in front of them; they then cautiously pulled themselves to their feet hand over hand, looking for all the world like eight monkeys on sticks, until eventually they were all standing. If the boat was not wobbling too furiously, then with a great flourish, off came their flower-garlanded boaters, for they too were dressed like sailors of a century before, and their hats had been decorated that morning by admiring sisters or even girlfriends. As they all lowered themselves carefully down again, the next boat came into sight, and the performance was repeated, until the complete flotilla of nine vessels had gone their way.

When darkness was falling, down we all trooped again to the riverside, where we enjoyed the most wonderful display of fireworks that I had ever seen, my experience up to then having been confined to a few rockets that we were allowed to let off at Wixenford.

I was only destined to enjoy that one peacetime Fourth of June, for in the autumn of that same year, the Great War broke out, and then there were quite different displays of fireworks to be seen in France, death-dealing ones, not the friendly display we had so much enjoyed from the banks of the River Thames.

During those war years, we went on celebrating the Fourth of June, but the celebrations grew progressively more austere. The procession of boats still took place – though I cannot remember them as I was elsewhere with my mother – but the crews did not dress up, they wore their grey flannel cricket trousers with rowing vests known as zephyrs. Instead of the members of the crew of each boat rising to their feet in succession, the crews of all nine boats stood up together – though I cannot for the life of me imagine what symbol of austerity this was meant to represent.

Harald Peake, one of my contemporaries, organised a potato patch on the lines of the 'Dig for Britain' campaign that was launched by Lord Woolton during the last war; apart from that, the school carried on in much the same way that it always had done. The only difference as far as I could see, apart from the fact that many young masters left to go into the armed services, older men being brought out of retirement to take their places, was that our futures were obscure. But it certainly was a sad and difficult time in which to have one's schooldays. Throughout the four years of the war, described as a 'war to end all wars', each of us was prepared, indeed expected, to die for our country. This was natural enough in consequence of the terrible casualty lists that we scanned in the newspapers each day. Indeed, seldom did a day pass without the name of a friend, relation or acquaintance appearing. To my own great grief, my half-brother, Maurice, my mother's eldest son, fell at Ypres on 13 May 1915.

The horrifying fact is that out of the nearly six thousand Etonians who served in the Great War, 1,160 were killed – about the same number as there were pupils – and a further 1,467 were wounded. I am proud to say that thirteen old Etonians won the Victoria Cross, 548 the Distinguished Service Order, and 744 the Military Cross.

It is a well-known fact that the casualties among young officers during the trench warfare were appalling – in fact, all that those young lives represented was cannon fodder – and naturally by sheer virtue of their birth and backgrounds, most Etonians received immediate commissions when they joined up. My final year at school, 1917–18 was summed up as a year in which there had been four Captains of the School and six Presidents of Pop, all of whom had left the school to go straight to the Front.

What I do find strange is that, although the school had always sent a team to compete in the rifle competitions at Bisley before the war – and they were to do so again during the 1920s – from 1914 to 1918 when I was at Eton, shooting was not even on the curriculum. Although the Bisley Meeting itself was not held during the war years, I would have thought that the fact that most boys were going to find themselves undergoing military training and service would have been sufficient reason to step up the shooting practice, rather than to cut it out altogether.

It had always been my full intention, war or no war, to go into the Army, as I have never had any doubts that what I wanted to do when I left school was to follow in my father's footsteps and go into the Blues, part of the Household Cavalry. Although I had joined the Army Class at the instigation of my parents, I needed no persuasion to continue and take the entrance examination for the Royal Military College at Sandhurst.

To get into the Blues, even during the war, it was necessary to pass an examination, which had to be quite a strict one, as the Regiment was always heavily over-subscribed. I took the exam before my eighteenth birthday and, much to my relief and not a little to my surprise, for I had never worked particularly hard at school, I found that I had passed with a high grade. I remember that my father was very pleased with me. But to our great annoyance, it was found that there had been a tiresome muddle over the dates, and the powers-that-be declared that I was too young, and therefore must stay on at school for another Half. Not only that, but to add insult to injury, I was required to sit the exam again. I was dreadfully disappointed, as I was longing to be able to get to the Front and have a go at the Boche, and in consequence I did not work at all. When I re-took the exam, although I did manage to scrape through, this time, much to my chagrin and to my parents' disappointment, my name appeared right at the bottom of the list.

All this had very far-reaching consequences for, had I gone into the Army in the spring of 1918, the odds were that my own name might well have figured on one of those terrible casualty lists that were the result of the severe fighting on the Western Front through the spring and summer eventually ending in decisive defeats of the enemy, and which brought the end of the war in sight.

Had I been killed, the Dukedom would have devolved on my father's next brother, and would have gone down through his family. By one of those strange quirks of fate, that is in fact what will happen, for my heir is my first cousin twice removed, David Somerset – himself the grandson of my father's next brother, Henry Richard Charles. David's elder brother, John, was killed in action on 15 April 1945, less than a month before the European war ended.

I was very sad when I left Eton, for I had had a happy five years there, during which I not only made friends who have lasted me a life-time, but I also learnt a great deal about self-discipline and even more about my fellow men.

All the same I was very eager to get on to the next part of my life and become a soldier.

CHAPTER THREE

ARMY LIFE

I spent a few days at Badminton after I left school and before I had to report at Sandhurst, but I found that I did not enjoy it as much as usual, for I could not wait to get on with my army training so that I could come to grips with the enemy at last. The time dragged until the day came for me to report at the Royal Military College, Sandhurst; and there they began training me to go into battle. However, the more I progressed with my training, the less likelihood there seemed to be of my having the chance of putting what I was learning into practice. In July and August of that summer, the tide of the war suddenly changed with the Combined Military Commanders, Marshal Foch of France, Field Marshal Haig of Great Britain and General Pershing of the United States, launching offensives on the Western Front of such intensity that by September, the German commanders were urging negotiations for peace.

I found the life at Sandhurst very different from that at Eton, the change being almost as great as the transition from private to public school. I now experienced a degree of freedom that had never before come my way throughout my eighteen years. Even though Eton has always been, relatively speaking, free and easy, unlike other public schools – certainly those of my time – nevertheless there were innumerable written and unwritten rules that governed the conduct and behaviour of the boys. So, having been steeped in that atmosphere for five years, I was scarcely prepared to plunge into a way of life where not only was I free to make most of my own decisions, but I was expected to do so. Naturally, I was required to do quite a lot of work and combat training, but at the same time, I was also able to play polo, to get home to hunt, and I also began building up a stable of my own horses.

The first hunter I ever bought on my own account came my way almost by accident. I was up at Rugby visiting Harry Rich who had been born at the Home Farm, Easton Gray, not many miles from Badminton, as I had heard that he had some useful polo ponies for sale. He said they were in a far-flung field and suggested that we should ride out to see them. A nice-looking chestnut called Robinstown, well up to my weight, was brought out for me; scarcely was I in the saddle than he took off, hardly giving me enough time to collect the reins together in my hands. Before I knew what had happened, we were soaring over an iron gate that led into the farmyard, and I pulled him up hard against the haybarn. I recognised his potential as a hunter, and when Harry Rich came running up, full of apologies for his horse's behaviour, I rather laughingly offered him £90 for the brute; so shocked was he at what had happened, that he accepted my offer on the spot. That horse turned out to be just about the best one I have ever bought; I had several hard seasons on him before I gave him to my wife soon after we were married, by which time he was a collected and experienced hunter, and she enjoyed many happy days mounted on his back.

I bought two other horses round about the same time; these came from the Army Remount Depôt at Nether Avon, just outside Bristol, where my Uncle Bill Harford, a serving officer there, advised me to go if I was looking for a bargain. One was called Oxo and cost me £70 and the other was Dunbar, for which I paid the princely sum of £40. They were two topping horses, and they also carried me extremely well. I remember that I enjoyed one of the best hunts of my life mounted on Dunbar; but towards the end of the run the poor devil got a stake through his chest while jumping a fence, and that was the end of him.

My time at Sandhurst flew by far too quickly, and I passed out well, to my great surprise and immense gratification, winning the coveted saddle that is presented to the best horseman. I used that saddle for many years; not until a few seasons ago, when the tree broke, did it come to the end of its useful life.

To win it I had to compete in a sort of 'Three-Day Event'. First, each of us was required to do a kind of dressage test that included all the exercises we had had to do hour after tedious hour in the indoor school. Next we were faced with a gruelling cross-country course, but that didn't really bother me, as I was well used to galloping hell-for-leather after my hounds, so I positively enjoyed it. The last test was a series of jumps that had been erected in the covered school. On looking back, I realise that the one big difference between that three-part test and the one facing eventers of today was that our mounts were allotted to us on the day. They came out of a hat, so to speak; we did not have the benefit of weeks of preparation and training on the horses that we were going to ride in the competition. Here again, I think I probably had an advantage over my competitors; although my hunters had certainly never had much training apart from their experience in the hunting field, I was quite accustomed to getting green horses into my own ways.

As you can imagine, my father was overjoyed by my win. He was not able to attend the passing-out ceremony as he had recently broken his leg and only moved about with the greatest of difficulty; but he showed his appreciation in the best possible way to my mind by sending me a handsome cheque.

While I was still officially at Sandhurst the Peace Treaties were signed at Versailles; although I had passed out of the Royal Military College, my Regiment had only lately returned from France, and was not yet ready to take me. All my life I have regretted the fact that I have never been able to bear arms for my King and country.

I well remember Armistice Day, for I happened to be up in London with a crowd of my Sandhurst friends, and we found ourselves crushed in a mighty throng of people that had gathered in the Mall and was surging down towards Buckingham Palace, where it was joined at the memorial to Queen Victoria in front of the Palace by further seething masses of people, all with the same thought in mind. They lifted their faces up towards the blank windows of that wide façade, and, joining together in a mighty roar, yelled at the tops of their voices: 'We want the King – we want the King!'

Pushed hither and thither, and so close to my fellow men that I could hardly breathe, I was thankful for my height, as it meant that I was able to see above the heads of most of the other people. I joined in with everybody else as they continued their chant: 'We want the King!' At long last the double glass doors leading to the Palace balcony were seen to move and the noise grew to a tremendous and ecstatic crescendo of cheers as the King and Queen came out and waved to the crowds.

They looked diminutive from where I stood, right in the centre of that vast crowd, but the overwhelming impression was that of mass loyalty to the Crown. The King and Queen were joined by other members of the Royal Family; and they stood out there waving to that great gathering of their subjects for several

9. *My mother and I attending the second polo test*
match between England and America, June 1921.

10. *A portrait of Mary painted by N. Becker, not long after we were married.*

minutes, before withdrawing once more into the Palace, the glass doors being closed behind them. Only then, slowly and reluctantly, did the enthusiastic crowd eventually disperse.

That mass display of emotion was extraordinarily moving. I have never forgotten the feeling of unity that existed for an hour or two between all those strangers from every walk of life who were drawn together by a common desire to show their love and loyalty to King and country, expressing it by their cheers.

I did not imagine for a moment that the next time such crowds would gather outside Buckingham Palace, I myself would be among the tiny figures on the balcony to be seen from afar, for my wife and I were staying with King George V and Queen Mary, who was her aunt, on the occasion of the Silver Jubilee in 1935. Then it was my turn to look down upon that great sea of anonymous faces that stretched far back up the Mall. Since then I have been on that balcony many, many times, but never have I been quite so moved as I was on Armistice Day, 11 November 1918.

At last the day dawned when my Regiment was quartered once more at its Albany Street Barracks, close to Regent's Park, and was ready to take me. First there came an interview with the Commanding Officer, Colonel Lord Tweedmouth. He was a man of fiery countenance, but with a heart of gold. About forty-five years old, he had served with great distinction in the South African War at about the time of my birth, and it was he who took the Regiment to France during the war that had just ended.

When I first set eyes on him, I thought I had never seen such a terrifying-looking man in the whole of my life. He was large and red, and he looked for all the world as if, should he become angry, he could quite easily swell up, turn purple and pop right out of his uniform. All the same, I thought that what he had to say to his new recruits made excellent sense, and his remarks appealed to me as being both straight from the shoulder and completely to the point.

He started by telling us that the men in the Regiment had had a hell of a time during the past five years, for they had fought right through the war in the thick of all the fiercest battles – the Guards Regiments have always been renowned for their valour and for their fighting qualities – and they had undergone all the horrors of trench warfare, the mud, the rats, the blood, the sweat, and all too often the sudden death.

He went on to say that all that was now over and we were

back in peacetime, so what he wanted us to do as young officers fresh to the task, was to help him to build up again the pre-war standards of both smartness and discipline – the twin foundations on which the well-deserved reputation of the Regiment had always been founded. He ended by saying that if we did not help him with his task, then he did not want to see us. After giving us a long, appraising look, he then turned on his heel and left the room.

I realise now that he showed his innate wisdom by appealing to us to help him, for being young, we were full of the vigour and enthusiasm of youth, and who could be better to help him with the job of pulling the Regiment together so that it could once more take pride of place in the British Army?

It did not take me long to discover that, in spite of his fiery countenance and abrupt manner, the Colonel was not only gifted in his understanding of the young, but also knew exactly how to bring out the best in those who were fortunate enough to serve under him.

I soon managed to establish a good relationship with him once I had had time to assess his fine qualities; even so, it was with some fear and trepidation that I went to him one day with a request. I asked him if I could take my annual leave in days, perhaps doing extra duties during the summer months, so that I could go down to Badminton twice a week during the hunting season to take out the pack of bitches that my father had recently given me, and which naturally I was aching to hunt. Lord Tweedmouth, fully aware of our family traditions, also knew that, to me, my hunting education was just as important as the one I was undergoing in the Army, and had no hesitation in granting my request.

So, on two separate days each week, I used to get up at the crack of dawn, shave and dress as swiftly as I could, and then race out of the barracks in time to hitch a lift on a mail van bound for Paddington. Once there, I caught a train that enabled me to get home in time to arrive at the Meet by 10.45 a.m. When the day's hunting was over, I managed to get back to barracks, even if not in time for dinner, at any rate, to report in before curfew.

In order to hunt hounds successfully, it is also necessary to be able to blow a horn competently, and I was fortunate enough to have a wonderful tutor. I often used to repair to the sound-proofed music-room at the barracks with Trumpet-Major Heggie, where he would give me lessons on a variety of brass instruments. I used to enjoy those sessions enormously, and so did he, for we fairly raised the roof with our cacophony of sound. I don't think there can ever have been anyone who played the bugle as well as the Trumpet-Major.

Our Army chargers were exercised in Regent's Park, and to get there we had to go fifty yards down Albany Street before turning into a lane leading directly to the park; but the road had been built with such a severe camber that we found it necessary to dismount for those fifty yards, for we were fearful of the horses falling and injuring their legs. When it was my turn to take the Guard down to Horse Guards Parade, I used to take a very unorthodox route. Instead of going straight down Portland Place and into Regent Street, I used to turn right and go along Wimpole Street, then left again, emerging into Oxford Street at the top of Bond Street; I was always sure to give my girlfriends good warning so as to be certain of a turn-out to see me riding at the head of my troop down that famous street with all its fashionable shops. What conceit!

During my five years at Eton and the first part of my time at Sandhurst, I had truly never been in the least aware of the charms of the opposite sex. I had been totally immersed in a man's world, and at the time, was completely happy to leave it at that. However things suddenly changed as soon as I was able to go to London whenever I liked, and started going to balls and dances. I dare say I would be considered a very late developer, nowadays, but I can assure you, I very soon made up for lost time, going from ball to ball, and making literally dozens of girlfriends.

Life for a young officer in the Household Brigade in those days was, in fact, one long round of pleasure for, not only were the duties enjoyable, but they were far from arduous. Leave was more than adequate, and I found that in spite of those extra duties I had undertaken, I was still able (during the summer months when there was no hunting) to get away most weekends to stay with friends.

In the early 1920s, most people were trying to have as good a time as possible, probably in an unconscious attempt to wipe out some of the horrific memories of the war years. I never found myself short of invitations, and each night I could have gone to at least three parties during the season; it was the same for all the young men who served with me. Values were very different in those days, and as my allowance had been stepped up considerably when I joined my Regiment, I found myself quite able to afford the champagne I could buy in nightclubs at £1 a bottle. We used to go on to one or other of them after dances, getting back to the barracks in time to snatch an hour or two of sleep before we had to spruce ourselves up to put in a smart appearance at early parade.

Such had been the shadow hanging over us as we grew up through the most formative years, that I think our obvious and totally understandable reaction was to live life to the full, the consequences be damned. I must add that, even though we played hard, we also worked very hard, and took an enormous pride in performing our regimental duties efficiently.

At the end of each summer when the Brigade's ceremonial duties had been completed, our bags were packed and we mounted our horses to ride right through west London, on across Surrey to the Guards' Camp at Pirbright. There we spent a month under canvas, the object of the exercise being not only to give our horses a much-needed rest after all their summer exertions, but also to give the young officers and the soldiers tuition and practice on the target ranges that lie at an angle to the more famous ones at Bisley. These ranges are so positioned that both groups of marksmen fire into the same danger area. It is obvious that shooting must play an important part in Army training, and we all thoroughly enjoyed having the chance to improve our aim with a rifle; for up to then most of us had been more proficient with a shotgun, with which we had all had more practice at home shooting game.

Our camp lay alongside the railway line, and we disliked the noise of the trains that rushed past us all through the night making a terrible racket. Several days later we realised how useful that line might prove to be. I dare say that during those first few days we needed to catch up with some of the sleep we had missed during the gaiety of the London season, but as the August days wore on, we started to get very bored in the evenings. Our thoughts turned wistfully to London and all its allures, where the season had not quite ended.

Those were the days before all young subalterns had cars, so we were entirely dependent on public transport or taxicabs. I cannot now remember who it was who had the bright idea – I wish I could say positively that it was me – that we should all board a train each evening after dinner which would swiftly carry us up to Waterloo in less than an hour. Once there, we were able to spend a happy time in the theatre or ball room before we had to race back to the station to catch a late train that would get us back to camp. And get us back to camp it certainly did! Taking it strictly in turns, as the train approached our camp one of us stood up and pulled the communication cord. All the brakes automatically came on, and the train shuddered to a halt right by the wire fence that separated the railway line from our camp. Before it came completely to a halt, out we all piled, leaving the culprit for that evening to stay behind and pay the £5 fine. We quickly swarmed over the wire fence, and there we were, back just in time to change before early morning reveille. How we managed to do all that without sleep and still get through the following day's exercises, I really don't know, but I suppose we were very young and resilient, and I dare say we snatched forty winks in the afternoons after luncheon.

It was not long before the soldiers cottoned on to what was happening, and they jumped on the bandwagon, for they too were naturally longing to go up to London to visit their wives and girlfriends. We turned a blind eye, and did not expect them to take their turn with the £5 fine. As far as I know, we were never found out. Certainly nothing was ever said.

I suppose that in the midst of all that very active life I must have been entertaining some thoughts of settling down right at the very back of my mind. During the hunting season of 1922–23 there appeared a new and very pretty face in the hunting field at home. This belonged to Lady Mary Cambridge, the second daughter of the Marquess of Cambridge. Her brother, Prince George of Teck, had just overlapped with me at Eton, and her aunt was Queen Mary, wife and consort of King George V.

Mary Cambridge was not only extremely pretty, but she was also an excellent horsewoman, and it was evident that she took a great interest in hound work, not coming out for the ride alone. So it is not surprising that she very soon caught my eye. She and a friend, Kathleen Crichton – one of Queen Mary's many God-daughters, a daughter of Viscount Crichton, sister of the future Earl of Erne, and later to become herself the Duchess of Abercorn – were staying for a few months at Sopworth House with some friends of ours, Algy and Molly Stanley, the idea being that they should enjoy a season's hunting with my father's hounds.

I suppose that Mary and I had what could only be called a whirlwind romance, for I proposed to her on 26 March, just before I was twenty-three, and she became my wife three months later, on 14 June 1923, two days after her birthday.

We were married in London and had a large and what was described in the gossip columns of the national press as a 'fashionable wedding' at St Margaret's, the church that stands right by the side of Westminster Abbey, where so many of our friends were married in those days.

Our wedding was attended by King George and Queen Mary, and also by Queen Alexandra, the Queen Mother. A special train-load of tenants came up from Badminton for the great occasion, and after the church ceremony, we had a huge reception at a house in Portland Place which was lent to us for the day. In common, I suspect, with most other bridegrooms, I cannot really say that I remember a great deal about my wedding day, except that at the end of it all, I felt as if I had shaken hands with half London. There were six bridesmaids, four of whom attended our Golden Wedding celebrations in 1973; my best man was Hugh Molyneux, later Earl of Sefton, whose father had been Master of the Horse from 1905 to 1907. Although Hugh was two years older than me, we had a lot in common, for we served in the Blues together and had played polo in the same team. He hunted with the Cottesmore, and was later to act as Field Master.

Just after the war, Hugh gave a dance for his twenty-first birthday at Croxteth, his home in Lancashire, where later I was to enjoy many wonderful days of grouse shooting; we once had a record bag of 993½ brace. One of my partners at that dance was Lady Elizabeth Bowes-Lyon. The wheel has certainly turned a full circle, for fifty years later, in the summer of our seventieth birthdays, Queen Elizabeth The Queen Mother, as of course she was destined to become, shared a dance with me given for us by the Queen at Buckingham Palace, and another one held at Windsor on our eightieth anniversaries. The first of these balls was also shared by my old friend, Dickie Mountbatten, Earl Mountbatten of Burma; had it not been for his tragic death at the hands of Irish terrorists the summer before, he too would have shared the Windsor dance.

Mary and I spent the first part of our honeymoon at Lowther Castle on the edge of the Lake District which was lent to us by my Godfather, Lord Lonsdale. As I said, he was better known, perhaps, as the Yellow Earl. The word 'yellow' was certainly not intended to be descriptive either of his character or of his courage, for nobody could possibly have had more of either, both in the hunting field where he shone, or in the boxing ring, where he vanquished. However, yellow was his favourite colour – this even extended to having canary-coloured cars.

From his hunting box at Oakham in Rutland he was Master of

the Woodland Pytchley from 1881 to 1885, taking that pack over when he was twenty-four years old. He was Master of the Quorn from 1893 to 1898, when he gave all his servants leather breeches, and the huntsman, Tom Firr, declared that never until then had he known what it was to be comfortable when hunting! My Godfather also kept a marvellous kennel of first-class terriers at the Quorn establishment. Later, following in the footsteps of his ancestor, the 1st Earl of Lonsdale, who was Master of the Cottesmore from 1788 to 1802, and indeed owned the hounds and brought them down by road at the beginning of each season from Lowther Castle, the Yellow Earl was Master of that fine pack of hounds for two periods: one from 1907 to 1911, and another that continued right through the Great War from 1915 to 1920 – he was forty-five at the outbreak of war, and therefore not needed for active service.

Once I was riding one of his horses when he was Master of the Quorn, and a stirrup leather broke when I was jumping a particularly hairy fence. Instead of sympathising with me in my predicament and apologising for the fact that I had been given a leather that could break, to my astonishment, he let the full force of his not inconsiderable fury loose on me, rating me right, left and centre. To his mind I should not have put so much weight on the leathers, and evidently no one had ever broken one before. I was simply terrified, and stood there absolutely tongue-tied while he harangued me. I continued the rest of the Hunt stirrupless, not daring to ask for another pair of leathers.

He was an extraordinarily colourful character and an all-round sportsman of the old-fashioned sort. He lived in great style at Lowther, and it is said that his family trustees made him an allowance of £84,000 a year, which he declared was not nearly enough. It certainly was not, as before the Great War, he managed to get through £4,000 a week! In London he had not one house, but two that stood side by side in Carlton House Terrace, overlooking the Mall and St James's Park, as he did not like having to go up more than one floor to get to his bedroom. He is reported to have said on meeting one of his neighbours, who, quite naturally, only had the normal quota of one house: 'But my dear man, wher*ever* do you sleep?'

When he died, I found that I was one of his executors, and it took me years to sort out the mass of debts that he left behind. However, he was always very generous to his Godchildren, and not only did he lend us his house for our honeymoon, but he also made me a life member of the MCC, and a life member of the

Royal Zoological Society – and, as I said before, he was always very generous with his tips.

Our honeymoon at Lowther Castle, which we had all to ourselves for a few days, was not very long, because we had been invited to stay later that month at Windsor for the Ascot races. My wife was George V's favourite niece and, after his only daughter, Princess Mary, the Princess Royal, was married to Lord Lascelles (later of course the Earl of Harewood) in the spring of 1922, the King called more and more upon my Mary to accompany him on various occasions. Indeed, that very summer after we were married, he invited her to go for a cruise with him aboard the Royal Yacht in the Mediterranean, but I was unable to go too because of the cub-hunting.

Each morning, before the races at Ascot started, a party started out from Windsor Castle to ride in the Park with the King. He had rather an unpredictable temper, and one of his little idiosyncrasies was that he never liked another horseman to pass him when he was riding. However, I remember that the Prince of Wales and I used to set off from behind him at a tangent, then making a great circle that took us right out in front of the King, but so far on that he was never aware that we had crossed his path. Jumping every obstacle that stood in our way, we finished up in our rightful places, dutifully riding behind the King once again. He must, I am sure, have wondered why our horses were blowing and sweating so much, but he never said anything.

When Mary and I eventually returned to Badminton after our honeymoon, we arrived by train at the station, to find the platform full of cheering people, and we were given a mighty welcome. My open car was waiting for us outside the station, and, although I took my place at the wheel, I was not permitted even to start the engine. Garlanded ropes had been attached to the axle by the tenants, and they drew us back to Badminton House in great style.

I had in fact bought that car in London a year or two before from a dealer in Great Portland Street, not far from the Albany Street Barracks. As in those days it was not necessary to take a test before one could drive a car, a friend drove me as far as Reading and I then took over and drove myself straight back to Badminton, without ever having had a single lesson, let alone a test.

The local celebrations for our homecoming went on far into that night, and there was dancing on the lawn in front of the house to the strains of music played by the Chipping Sodbury Quarry Band. It was a free-for-all and people came from miles around to join in the fun. There were a hundred and forty-two names on the list of those people in our service who subscribed to two armchairs and a rosebowl for our wedding present.

When we were first married, we settled down in The Cottage, a nice house situated at the entrance to the drive that leads to the Kennels. My heir, David Somerset and his wife, Caroline, a daughter of the Marquess of Bath, live there now with their family Harry, Anne, Eddy and Johnnie. Although it is called The Cottage it is really quite a nice-sized family house, though it is tiny compared with Badminton House. I must admit that during the short time we lived there I did feel a trifle cramped, having been accustomed all my life to the spaciousness of the far bigger house.

Alas, our cottage existence was not destined to continue for more than a year or two. At the beginning of the hunting season of 1924, when we had only been married for sixteen or seventeen months, my father went down with what was to prove to be his last illness, though he had been ailing for some time. He had not been able to hunt for several years, as he had become very heavy; even so, he used to follow hounds like his grandfather before him, not in a carriage drawn by skewbald ponies, but in a chauffeur-driven open car, and accompanied by a pet dog that used to wear a smart coat in Blue and Buff.

My wife also used to take out a little terrier that wore a similar coat, and to her horror one never-to-be-forgotten day, when he saw the fox running across an open field, he struggled so much that she was obliged to let him go. Off he sped, and accounted for that fox before ever a hound appeared on the scene. There he stood, the obvious culprit, a smug expression on his face and wearing the Blue and Buff!

My father's death marked the end of an epoch, and I freely admit that the day he died, 27 November 1924, was the saddest one of my whole life.

An account of my father's funeral read as follows:

From the wooded Cotswolds and the bleak Mendips – from the forests of Cirencester and Braydon to the Lower Woods – from the Thames and the source of the Avon to the Severn and the sea – there was no sound of the horn, no music of hounds in cry, no thudding and scudding and squelching of galloping hoofs, in all the land – because he who loved the chase so deeply and was the greatest of foxhunters had passed to his long rest . . .

My emotions were very mixed when, a few days later, I rode on to the Meet at Leighterton. It was a very moving and important occasion for me, as it was the first time I had hunted my own hounds as Duke of Beaufort. I am pleased to say we started with a very good hunt, a seven-mile point, killing the fox in the open.

CHAPTER FOUR

BADMINTON: THE HOUSE

To say that I love Badminton is, of course, true, but the fact is that my feeling for the place goes far deeper than love, for it penetrates right into the very fibres of my being, and I am never really happy when I am away from it for more than a day or two at a time. Even then, I telephone every day to see if everything is all right. I suppose it could be summed up as a permanent love affair, as the Badminton Estate and all that it stands for, not only in the way of sport which is my way of life, but also for the livelihood and well-being of my family, has always formed the basis of my very existence.

A house like Badminton is not just a pile of bricks and mortar. It is a living testimony to the people who have gone before: all those who have been born, lived, loved, been happy, suffered and died within the safety of its walls and under the shelter of its roof.

The actual house, although giving the appearance of a whole, is in fact a conglomerate of periods, for, like so many other English houses of a similar type, it has evolved over the years, reflecting not only the history of the family, but also of its fortunes.

The roots of our family are in Wales, where we have had property since the time of the 1st Earl of Worcester. He was acknowledged to be the illegitimate son of Henry Beaufort, Duke of Somerset, and therefore took the surname Beaufort from his father. In about 1508, Charles Beaufort married Elizabeth Herbert, the only daughter and heiress of William Herbert, Earl of Huntingdon and Baron Herbert of Raglan, Chepstow and Gower. She brought with her not only vast estates that centred on Raglan, but also the Herbert title which goes down in the female line. When her father died, she assumed the title of Baroness Herbert, and it was as Lord Herbert that my ancestor was summoned to Parliament when Henry VIII came to the throne. He was later created Earl of Worcester by King Henry as a reward for services to the Crown.

Raglan Castle where they lived, and their descendants after them, was destroyed by Oliver Cromwell, though it was gallantly defended by the 5th Earl of Worcester, who was advanced to the dignity of Marquess on 2 March 1642 by Charles I. However, the Welsh estates remained in the possession of the family for many more years until some were sold in the last century; but I still have thousands of acres of land in the principality, mostly woodland where I have planted over a million trees. In fact it is the revenue from that land which enables us still to live at Badminton. Wales has always been very dear to my heart and I myself pay regular visits to the country. Each year a bus load of Welsh people travel across the Avon Bridge to spend a day with us at Badminton, where we revive the old practice of holding a Court Leat in the house. This is a traditional meeting, and we have had many enjoyable parties that end with a dinner and a sing-song, much enjoyed by our melodious Welsh guests.

In 1601, the 4th Earl of Worcester was made Master of the Horse by Queen Elizabeth I in succession to the Earl of Essex, who by then had fallen out of her favour, and Worcester was to continue in this office for the following fifteen years. Not only was he Master of the Horse, but he was also a Privy Councillor and a joint Commissioner for the office of Earl Marshal on seven occasions; in that capacity he was a member of the body that tried and condemned Guy Fawkes.

Before ever I knew about my ancestor's connections with the infamous Guy Fawkes, I copied the following into one of my notebooks:

> Please to remember
> The Fifth of November
> The Gunpowder, Treason and plot.
>
> I see no reason
> Why the Gunpowder Treason
> Should ever be forgot.
>   (old nursery rhyme)

Worcester was Earl Marshal at the Coronation of King James I and Lord Chamberlain at King Charles I's Coronation in 1625. He was Commissioner of the Treasury from 1626 until his death in 1628.

With all those official duties to fulfil in London, it is not surprising that he looked for a property about halfway between his Welsh home at Raglan and the capital. It was not long before he found the manor of Great Badminton which he bought from Nicholas Boteler in 1608. Badminton had belonged to the Boteler family for more than four hundred years, so it has had only two owners in seven hundred years.

When the 4th Earl died, he left the Badminton estate to his younger son, Thomas, who was created Viscount Somerset of Cashel in Co. Tipperary. But it was destined to return to the head of the family, as Thomas's only daughter, Elizabeth, died, without having any children, and bequeathed Badminton back to Henry, 3rd Marquess of Worcester who later became the 1st Duke of Beaufort.

Of that original house where the Botelers had lived for so many years, and which was described as 'a fayre stone howse', all that positively remains now is a huge room that we call the Old Kitchen. Standing on the extreme south-west corner of the present-day house, this must originally have been the great hall of the Tudor mansion; this is shown, not only by the height of the ceiling, but also by the unevenness of the tiles on the roof and by the massive chimney-piece. The Old Kitchen still performs a useful function, for we hold parties in it, and its walls, that are hung with antlers and below those are copper saucepans bearing the family crest, which were in daily use when I was a boy, often reverberate with the sound of the old hunting songs that we roar out on occasions such as the Court Leat Dinner and the annual Earth Stoppers' Feast.

My favourite is, I think:

Here's to the fox, in his earth below the rocks,
And here's to the line that we follow,
And here's to the hound with his nose upon the
                                        ground,
So merrily we whoop and we holloa!

Chorus
Then drink puppy, drink, and let every puppy drink,
That is old enough to lap and to swallow,

For he'll grow into a hound,
So we'll pass the bottle round,
And merrily we'll whoop and we'll holloa!

(old hunting song)

The Old Kitchen is also put to good use during our Three-Day Event each April when it is used as a canteen for grooms and other visitors, and I am told that the food served there rivals that of my own kitchen.

English noblemen throughout the ages have frequently fancied themselves as amateur architects, and judging by the scores of beautiful great houses that throng our countryside, they have proved remarkably successful.

My ancestor, Henry Somerset, 1st Duke of Beaufort, was no exception. He inherited Badminton in 1655 when he was still Lord Herbert, having returned five years earlier from exile in the Low Countries; he had left his parents in Holland sharing a house with Charles II. His father, the 2nd Marquess of Worcester, was a scholar, and while in exile carried out various scientific experiments; after he returned to this country he published a paper (1663) which showed that he fully understood the power and application of the principles of the steam engine – long before Stephenson was born.

On Henry Herbert's return to this country in 1650, one of the first things he did was to join the Protestant Church. This was a very wise move, for not only did it ensure his own safety, but it also enabled him to get Cromwell's blessing on his inheritance of Badminton five years later. Cromwell directed his Attorney General to

> prepare a grant for Henry Lord Herbert of Ragland and his heirs to a park or parks at Badminton . . . within his several Manors of Great Badminton and Little Badminton in our Countie of Gloucester and his several lands and grounds that is to say within the land or wood grounds commonly called Swangrove and other grounds thereto adjoining containing by estimation Two hundred acres more or less situated and being within our said Countie of Gloucester and the wood grounds commonly called Allengrove adjoining situate and lying within our countie of Wiltshire.

Fortunately Henry Herbert had married a woman who came from a very celebrated family of gardeners, the Capels. It was her father who had made a famous garden on the site of the present Kew Gardens, and said to be too sour to grow anything! Lovely houses cannot rest on their beauty alone, for like beautiful women, and gems for that matter, they require a suitable setting; from a giant plan that we still have at Badminton, it can be seen that the setting that was planned for Badminton must have rivalled many of its contemporaries in Europe. Entitled 'Badminton the Duke of Beaufort His House' it is not so much the house that at first sight appears to be illustrated, but the outline of the formal gardens that were to surround it, though it has never been absolutely certain that those gardens were ever completed. I imagine that a sophisticated aerial survey might give the answer to that question. My ancestress, Mary Capel, widow of Lord Beauchamp by whom she had a son who later became 3rd Duke of Somerset, herself illustrated a unique and most beautiful book of rare plants and flowers which we bring out from time to time to show to visitors who are interested in such things.

I am fascinated to see that even in those far off days, animals evidently played an important part in the daily lives of the family, as we find from a numbered index to that great plan; on it are marked not only the parlours, drawing-rooms, Church and Chapel, with a host of workrooms and stores for the plumber, the chandler, the joiner, the soap boiler and the carpenter, but also equally fine accommodation for the greyhounds and dogs, with 'styes' for the pigs, runs for 'ginny piggs' and poultry, and an aviary for the birds.

The 1st Duke must have been what I can only describe as a compulsive builder, for he remodelled Badminton, while working on two other projects at the same time: Great Castle House at Monmouth, and Troy House. Troy House had belonged to the Somersets since the 3rd Earl of Worcester bought it, from the James family in 1584 not very long before he died; it stands about a mile outside the town of Monmouth, and is now a Convent.

He spent the second half of his life enlarging and enriching these various houses, turning Badminton from that 'fayre stone howse' into a much larger and far more imposing residence, so that it would be fit to entertain a king. Sadly there is no record that Charles II ever came to Badminton, though it is known that he took the waters at nearby Bath. However, Queen Anne came to a feast at Badminton on her way from Cirencester to Bath in the time of the 2nd Duke. Charles II, though declaring that the family fully deserved to be given a dukedom for all the soldiers they had raised and the money they had given to his cause, did not carry out his promise until 1682, twenty-two years after the Restoration.

The 1st Duke's knowledge of physics, mathematics, and architecture must have been a little sketchy, as is evidenced to this day, for there are many inexplicable little gaps in the house that have either been filled in or covered over. I think there can be little doubt that one of the secrets of that old-time army of amateur architects was that they must surely have employed first-class master builders who saw to it that, at any rate, the work carried out was professionally sound, even if they were not permitted to alter the plans and remedy the defects.

Lord Guilford who was an almost exact contemporary of King Charles II, a distant kinsman by marriage of the 1st Duke, and one of the most prominent lawyers in England, in spite of the fact that he was a mere forty-eight years old when he died in the same year as the King, paid a visit to the house which he described graphically, saying that the Duke had a 'princely way of living' which was

> . . . above any other, except crowned heads that I have
> notice of in Europe, and in some respects greater than
> most of them.

He went on to say that the Duke had more than £2,000 per annum in his hands – an enormous sum in those days – with which he managed a great part of the country around Badminton, employing stewards, bailiffs and other servants to this end.

The 1st Duke evidently bred all his own horses; apparently he hardly ever had an old favourite put down, but provided a sort of home of rest for those that remained fit, even if they could no longer work. Quite apart from a block of stables that he built for his own use, which were not rebuilt until my grandfather's time (with money raised by the sale of my father's Commission in the Blues in 1875), he provided stabling for forty horses behind 'a neat dwelling-house' called the Inn, which was where he lodged his visitors' servants and their horses.

He had about two hundred members of his household to provide for, and to this end there were nine dining-tables at Badminton:

> . . . and for the accommodation of so many a large hall
> was built with a sort of alcove at one end for distinc-
> tion, but yet the whole lay in view of him that was chief

Returning from our Honeymoon June 1923.

11. On our return to Badminton station after our honeymoon, the tenants attached ropes to my car and drew us to Badminton House.

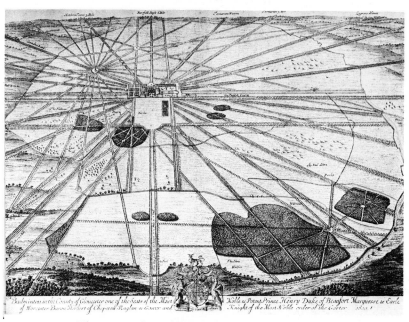

12. The 1600 plan of Badminton showing Swangrove at bottom right.

13. *Painting of the North Front of Badminton House, one of two Canalettos commissioned by the 4th Duke.*

14. *The West Front seen from the orchard on the other side of the duck pond. The old laundry was on the left and in my childhood the fire engine was kept in the old brewery on the right.*

... The tables were properly assigned, as, for example, the chief stewards with the gentlemen and pages, the master of the horse with the coachmen and liveries, and under steward with the bailiffs and some husband-men, the clerk of the kitchen with the bakers, brewers and all together and other more inferior people under these in places apart.

The women, too, had their own dining-room where the Duchess was attended by her chief woman with the gentlewomen, the housekeeper with the maids, and so on down the female scale.

What a vivid picture that all conjures up, in spite of being couched in such old-fashioned language!

Every morning of her life, just like my own mother, the Duchess used to make a tour of inspection, visiting every corner of the house and if she

... observed anything amiss or suspicious as a servant riding out or the like, nothing was said to that servant, but his immediate superior or one of a higher order was sent for, who was to inquire and answer if leave had been given or not. If not, such servant was straight turned away. No fault of order was passed by, for it may be concluded that there are enough of these that pass undiscovered.

My ancestor had planned great vistas for his new and wonderful house; evidently he was helped in his task by the people who lived round-about, for

... divers of the gentlemen cut their trees and hedges to humour his vistas, and some planted their hills in his lines for compliment at their own charge.

The Duke was Lord Lieutenant of four or five counties and Lord President of Wales; he must have had to entertain on a very large scale, and he evidently took these entertaining duties very seriously, for Lord Guilford reported that breakfast was in the gallery that opened into the gardens,

... then perhaps a deer was to be killed, or the gardens or parks with the several sort of deer to be visited, and if it required mounting, horses of the Duke's were brought for all the company.

Times have evidently not changed all that much in the three hundred ensuing years, for I also take my guests around the Park to see my deer, and I also mount them for a day's hunting whenever I can, though I cannot, alas, emulate my grandfather who is said to have mounted seventeen friends.

> ... The ordinary pastime of the ladies was in a gallery on the other side, where the Duchess had divers gentlewomen commonly at work upon embroidery and fringe-making, for all the beds of state were made and furnished in the house.

Those so-called 'beds of state' are still in use to this day, and although they now contain more up-to-date mattresses than the original ones made of horsehair, their hangings are as beautiful as they were when hung originally straight from the embroidery needles of those talented seventeenth-century 'divers gentle-women'.

When the 1st Duke died in 1699, he was succeeded by his grandson, for his only son had been killed only the year before in a coaching accident on a corner of the road near Troy House. I often drive round this corner on the way home after I have been fishing on the Wye, where I own a beat that runs from the town of Monmouth to just beyond what used to be a viaduct. My ancestors once owned the fishing rights on the whole of the River Wye; sadly my grandfather gave the whole lot to the Crown after four of his ghillies had been killed by poachers, as he felt that he no longer wanted the responsibility. The mind boggles when one considers what those rights would be worth nowadays!

As it is, I can leave Badminton at nine o'clock in the morning, having dealt with my post, and be waist-deep in the river not much more than an hour later.

Behold the Fisherman
He riseth early in the morning and disturbeth the
               whole household.
Mighty are his preparations.
He goeth forth full of hope, and when the day
  is far spent, he returneth smelling of strong
  drink, and the truth is not in him.

The 2nd Duke was fifteen when he succeeded his grandfather; he died at the early age of thirty, but not before he had been married three times. His elder son, Henry, by his second wife, Lady Rachel Noel, daughter of the Earl of Gainsborough (who herself died in childbirth when their second son, Charles Noel was born), became the 3rd Duke of Beaufort at the age of seven. Both the little boys were therefore orphaned and brought up by guardians. The 3rd Duke, Henry, was destined to bring about many more changes at Badminton. When he was nineteen, he and his brother, who was two years younger, were sent on a Grand Tour of Europe with their tutor, a Mr Philips, as was the common custom in noble families of that time. It was undoubtedly during that prolonged expedition that the tastes of both the brothers were formed; they returned to Badminton with many fine pictures that hang on the walls to this day, and a host of other rare treasures and objéts d'art.

Among the pictures that are still at Badminton brought back from this Grand Tour is one reputed to be by Leonardo da Vinci, for which the 3rd Duke paid the magnificent sum of four hundred crowns, then about £200. He must have acquired this in Italy under the guidance of two of his Uncle Ormonde's friends, the Cardinals Alberoni and Albani, names that were to be conjured with in Italy at that time. His uncle was the Marquess of Ormonde who had married Mary, daughter of the 1st Duke. From France he brought two pictures by Claude and two by Nicholas Poussin; he brought a picture by Michael Angelo Americi, known as Caravaggio, leader of the Neapolitan school of painting in the late sixteenth century, and one by another Neapolitan, Salvator Rosa. He also had himself painted by Trevisani.

There is a bit of a mystery about some of the things that the 3rd Duke undoubtedly bought in Italy, for although he knew full well that they had been despatched, they did not turn up among the packing cases that eventually arrived at Badminton some months after the two brothers had returned. However, in that strange way in which fate sometimes seems to work, when he was glancing through a catalogue of a sale of objéts d'art that was to take place in Poland Street, London, he found what were undoubtedly descriptions of things that were missing from his European consignment of goods. Even more strange to relate, Mr Philips, his erstwhile tutor, who had recently retired and who had shared the brothers' journeyings, was now living in Poland Street. I don't find it altogether surprising that Philips was not available for cross-examination, his excuse being that he was suffering from gout.

Not only did he bring back treasures, but the young Duke also returned from Europe with his head full of new ideas for re-modelling the house his grandfather had built of stone exca-vated from a quarry still to be found between Doddington and Acton Turville. Although this quarry is now hidden from sight by a huge clump of trees planted by one of my forebears as a covert, there is still to be seen the sealed entrance to a passage that goes underground as far as an airshaft a mile away, which is where the stone ends. There is a story that this tunnel leads right into the house itself, but I am quite sure there is no truth in this rumour – for one thing there is no evidence of any such tunnel in the house; for another, the house was built a couple of hundred years too late to need a hiding hole or escape route for Roman Catholic priests on the run from Henry VIII. Also, Cromwell, tyrant that he was, was dead and buried by the time the rebuild-ing had been completed.

So in 1730, when he was twenty-three, my ancestor, the 3rd Duke asked William Kent, the painter-turned-architect who was responsible for the Horse Guards Building in Whitehall, and Holkham Hall, the Norfolk home of the Earls of Leicester, to come to Badminton, to re-design the North Front, and also to complete the West Front, to add a third storey to the East Front, and to design the present entrance to the house and the entrance to the Park. It is thought that he also employed Kent's friend, the celebrated landscape architect, Capability Brown, to sweep away the formal gardens, however large they may or may not have been in extent, that had been laid out by his great-grandfather and his Capel great-grandmother. These were replaced by the cunningly planted woods and thickets that, when fully grown, blend into the general landscape, making even distant hills appear part of a garden that was planned in this way. This is a totally English characteristic, far removed from the formal landscaping of the grand gardens that are a feature of France, Germany, Austria and Italy. Little temples and grottoes formed part of the general plan, but alas, they have vanished over the years.

When he had finished tidying up the amateur architecture of the 1st Duke, William Kent then turned his attention to the design and ornamentation of an ornate and beautiful little build-ing known as Worcester Lodge that lies at the top end of the three-mile-long avenue of trees stretching out to the north of the house. Taking the form of a gateway, over its arch is a lovely room known as the summer dining-room. This has often been the scene of family parties in the past, and I sometimes use it nowadays for my shooting luncheons. The rest of my shooting luncheons take place in a little iron hut, heated by an old stove, and hung with calendars and decorations much cherished by my head forester, Charlie Chappell, some of which have to be taken down if we are to have ladies present. Talk about the sublime to the ridiculous!

The summer dining-room at Worcester Lodge is beautifully proportioned with five great windows and a balcony, with superb plaster work on the ceiling, only equalled to my mind by that, also designed by William Kent, for our Front Hall. While Kent was carrying out all this work, the 3rd Duke commissioned John Wootton to paint five magnificent equestrian pictures for the Front Hall, which was also being re-designed and redecorated right down to the very picture frames by William Kent.

Before John Wootton embarked on his mammoth task the Duke – perhaps at Kent's instigation, for he too had been sent to Rome to complete his artistic education by a patron some years before – sent him to Rome so that he could gain the necessary training and experience. It took him several years to complete the canvases, during which time he lived at Badminton.

Kent did not touch the beautiful oak staircase that the 1st Duke had put in going right from the bottom to the top of the house, nor did he move the Grinling Gibbons carvings that decorate our dining-room. The latter task was done by my wife, who rearranged them in such a clever way that they are now shown to far better advantage.

William Kent's design transformed the outside of the house, for although it was evidently imposing in its original state as designed by the 1st Duke, under Kent's skilled hand it acquired an elegance that had hitherto been lacking; this is shown to perfection in one of the two pictures of Badminton by Canaletto that were commissioned by Charles Noel, the 4th Duke, and hang in our drawing-room today.

The 3rd Duke, who did so much for Badminton House to make it into the place we love today, died when he was only thirty-eight. As he had no children, he was succeeded by his younger brother, Charles Noel, who, as I have said, commissioned the two magnificent Canaletto paintings. In the foreground of the one that depicts William Kent's new North Front some rather stylised deer are seen prominently displayed running across the picture.

Deer have always been a feature of our park, and were indeed the main prey for the hounds in those days, though they have not been hunted at Badminton for more than two hundred years. I still have two herds, one of about fifty fallow deer, and the other about two-hundred strong of red deer. Although most great parks have a herd of fallow deer, red deer are seldom to be seen in park surroundings today, for they are mostly to be found in their wild habitat in and around the moorlands of Devon and Somerset, where they are still hunted with hounds, and in the Scottish highlands where they are stalked and shot with rifles. Both sports require great skill and a high degree of patience and knowledge of venery.

People who are accustomed to getting only the briefest and almost always unexpected glimpses of red deer in their natural surroundings, never fail to be amazed when they see mine. Although by no means tame, it is possible to ride a horse, or even to drive a Land-Rover, which I frequently do when we have guests who show interest in the deer, quite close enough to be able to study them with the naked eye, and without recourse either to a telescope or to field-glasses. They are magnificent specimens, and each year the spread of their antlers grows wider and wider, with more and more points. Sometimes we pick up the old horns in the Park where they have been cast in the spring; I am afraid to say that these are generally sold, as they fetch a lot of money, especially in the United States.

One of the big problems with keeping deer in captivity is to make sure that, while being confined within a certain area, they are at the same time provided with sufficient room to move about at will. We have had to put up a very high deer-proof fence right around the perimeter of the Park; but because they are thus not free to roam in their constant search for food nearly as far as they would if they were wild, we have to feed them in the winter. This has its advantages though, for as April approaches, my keeper feeds them further and further away from the house, so that they become accustomed to remaining in the far corner of the Park, and are therefore not disturbed or frightened by the enormous crowds that throng the Park at the time of the Three-Day Event.

Since my seventieth birthday, I have had the opportunity of learning more about the art of stag-hunting, this coming about through an invitation I received from Mr Bob Nancekivel who was then joint Master of the Devon & Somerset Staghounds. He asked me to go down and judge their young entry of hound puppies, a visit which was followed up with an invitation to have a day's stag-hunting.

The Meet on that occasion was on Winsford Hill, and it served to bring back a host of old memories. Long ago, when I was only twenty-one, there was such a severe drought at Badminton that we could not start cub-hunting because the ground was too hard, so, together with a few friends, I went down to Exmoor to enjoy a few days of hunting down there. By one of those strange coincidences that often seem to happen, my first day's stag-hunting – now nearly sixty years ago – was from Winsford Hill. And on that day the stag obligingly ran almost back to Minehead where we were staying.

Not only did we stag-hunt and fox-hunt, but we also played polo in the evenings on the polo ground at the foot of the cliff on which the ancient Dunster Castle (home of the Luttrell family for many generations), stands as a sentinel overlooking the Bristol Channel towards Wales. That polo ground went just before the war, and reverted to meadows which are now the scene of an annual Agricultural Show, one of the highlights of local life.

I was introduced to the pleasures of polo by my father. He had enjoyed the game when he was in the Blues, and on 7 June 1874 was a member of the winning team that initiated the playing of the game at Hurlingham. This historic match was between the Blues and the 1st Life Guards; it was watched by the Prince and Princess of Wales (later King Edward VII and Queen Alexandra), the Duke and Duchess of Edinburgh (Queen Victoria's second son and his bride who was one of the daughters of the Tsar), the Duke of Connaught, and Queen Mary's father, the Duke of Teck. Polo had only recently been brought to England from India, and it was described in a newspaper report of June 1874 as 'This newly-imported Oriental pastime, which may be called "hockey on horseback"'.

When being taken on one of my conducted tours round the Park, my visitors often comment on a small, slightly ramshackle, log-built hut which is tucked away behind the Mount Pond. This funny little house was built by one of my ancestors entirely for the diversion and entertainment of his guests. When he was taking people for a drive around the Park, he would draw their attention to this log hut, and drive towards it. As the intrigued party approached, out of the door would jump a 'hermit' clad in rags. This hermit was in fact only one of the second footmen who had been sent out to the hut to don his ragged outfit and make his surprise appearance for the amusement of the house-party staying at Badminton at the time. I do hope that they were generous with their tips to make it a job that was sought after by the young footmen!

For many years now it has been my habit to drive up the Park on a Sunday morning to have a consultation with my head forester, Charlie Chappell, who has worked for me and my family for more than forty years. Together we inspect work that has been carried out during the previous week, and plan what needs to be done in the future.

Although, unlike my ancestors, my building activities have been minimal, being confined to maintaining the structure of the house, what I have done has been to carry out a forestry programme on a very large scale. Where forestry and trees are concerned, the future is the all-important thing that has to be borne in mind constantly. We are now able to enjoy the beautiful English landscape because our ancestors planted trees with vision and foresight, many of the forests and woods that they planned and planted two or three hundred years ago having only reached full maturity during the course of this century.

What I have tried to do is to emulate the imaginative foresight of my ancestors, so that perhaps in a further two or three hundred years, people who enjoy the fruit of my labours will have reason to thank me.

During the past few years when I have been planning my forestry programme, I have never allowed myself to forget the profound effect of the dreaded Dutch Elm disease on our general landscape; in fact it must have come second only in its effect to the Enclosure Acts of the eighteenth century that divided the countryside into the fields that are part and parcel of the look of the land. Because of this, I now utilise a range of trees, and avoid favouring one or two species, while, at the same time, trying to continue to follow the essentially English landscape tradition that has always produced subtle shades and shapes that suit our soft light and gentle climate.

Although I was devastated when we had to take down our precious and prized elms all over the Park, I agree with a comment made by the Director of the Tree Council, Christopher Dodd, who said that the decline of the elm has not been a prick to action, but has served as a goad. At Badminton we have been literally forced into a tree-planting programme of such magnitude that it might easily have been postponed – and in the normal course of events, it would certainly have been spread out over a far longer period of time. In this case I think it is true to say that some good has come out of evil.

I have always had a policy of the commercial coppicing of small and often neglected woodland areas, for these, by careful planning, can be made to produce a good yield in what is a comparatively short time. I try to buy up any such pieces of woodland within the perimeter of my estate or on its boundaries that come on to the market. These not only provide us with additional coverts for hunting, but they can also be turned into money-making acres. We sell a good deal of our wood for top-class furniture making, and now that wood-burning stoves are all the vogue with the cost of other fuels soaring higher and higher, I know that we will have a long-term market for the wood not good enough either for factory use or for pit-props.

When I am planting a tree for commemorative purposes – and we do quite a lot of that at Badminton – I not only see to it that plants with strong and fibrous root systems are chosen so that they will take readily to their new environment, but I also see to it that three such trees are planted. This is an insurance policy that nearly always pays off, for out of the three, one may well die from natural causes, another may be destroyed by vandals, but the odds are that the third will survive and flourish.

Apart from my forestry activities, I have also taken a great interest in all the farming activities that are carried out on the Estate, one of my few regrets – and I do not have many! – being that I never found the time to do an agricultural course, however short. Farming is so technical today, that a proper training is really a necessity for anyone who wants to make a good living out of the land.

Badminton has for some years now been run as a family company with me and my heir, David Somerset, being partners, and to this end, his eldest son, Harry Somerset, did a comprehensive course at Cirencester Agricultural College, so I am full of hope for the future.

Houses such as Badminton are part and parcel of our English heritage, and that being so, it is the solemn duty of those who are fortunate enough to have them to do their best to see that they are handed down in good condition for posterity. That has always been my aim and my ambition.

CHAPTER FIVE

HUNTING AND MY ANCESTORS

My love of the chase comes from the thrill and challenge of a ride across country; from the skill and effort of a good pack of hounds; of the pleasure of riding an experienced or promising horse; and especially from the cry of the hounds, from the sound of the horn, from a good holloa, and from the hours spent riding in a green countryside. (From an interview I once gave.)

When I was still in the Blues, and a couple of years before I had even met my wife, who, as I have said, was King George's favourite niece, I was invited to shoot at Sandringham. Although I had always been accustomed to mixing with people at all levels, as I had had to do so all my life, nevertheless I still found it a little daunting at the age of twenty-one to be placed in the shooting line between two of the finest shots in the world, George V himself and Sir Harry Stonor, who was Deputy Master of the Royal Household at that time. I am thankful to say that I did not disgrace myself, and was invited again!

To a great degree I had to thank Fred Young, the keeper who had instilled in me twelve years before a deep-lying and long-lived love of shooting, for it was really to his encouragement and help that I owed my degree of skill with firearms. On that first visit to Sandringham I was asked to bring a loader; of course I took Fred as my loader and my valet. He was a fine figure of a man, and one evening during my stay, the King made a little wager with me, declaring that his own valet had the finer set of calves. Both men were sent for and, rather sheepishly, were required to present their legs for measurement. Sad to relate, the King's entrant won that contest by about a millimetre!

On the final day of that first visit of mine to Sandringham, the

King turned to Fred Young and said: 'Of course, Young, you realise that our lives at Sandringham revolve around the shooting?'

Completely at his ease, Fred Young remained unawed and apparently totally unaffected by the fact that he was being called upon to address his Monarch. He quickly doffed his cap and his answer came just as fast: 'Yes, Sir, I do. And of course our lives at Badminton revolve around the hunting.'

Those words summed up the whole situation in a nutshell, for it is true to this day to say that the lives of everyone at Badminton revolve around the hunting, and have done so for generations. Somebody once said that in order to write a history of hunting, it would be necessary to write a history of my hounds.

We have trustworthy records in our archives of the pack of hounds that has been kept at Badminton since 1728 in the time of the 3rd Duke; in those days it was hardly ever the fox but generally the hare and often the stag that were the quarry. Early records show that two packs of hounds were kept, one being used for hare-hunting and the other solely for the pursuit of the stag. Those harriers were the old-fashioned light-coloured ones which are still to be found in a few packs nowadays, and our records of 1734 show that, while there were thirty couple of harriers, there were only six couple of deerhounds, the two being distinct and separate breeds of hound. However, six years later, by 1740, the deerhound pack had been very much enlarged, the two packs being more or less equal in number, thus showing that the 3rd Duke was evidently becoming more and more keen on stag-hunting. As he had recently been separated from his wife, whom he subsequently divorced – a terrible scandal in those days – I wonder if he had turned to sport for consolation? Round about the same time that he increased the number of his hounds, he abandoned hare-hunting altogether, entering his harriers to the fox – though stag-hunting was also abandoned at Badminton in favour of the fox in the next generation.

The 3rd Duke only lived for two years after his divorce, dying in 1745 at the early age of thirty-eight while he was taking the waters at Bath. He left no children, so the title therefore went to his younger brother, Charles Noel (named for their mother, a daughter of the Earl of Gainsborough, whose family surname is Noel). Since then the dukedom has come down for six generations in a direct line from father to son.

The 4th Duke only outlived his brother by eleven more years, and he also died at a comparatively early age – forty-seven. When he was thirty-one he married Elizabeth Berkeley, who was Baroness Bottetourt in her own right, so she brought that strange title into the family to join the Herbert one that goes down through the female line. They had one son and five daughters; it was that son, Henry, who changed the hunting history of Badminton.

The story told in our family is that the 5th Duke of Beaufort who succeeded his father when he was only twelve years old, was returning one day some six years later in about 1762, after a disappointing and unsuccessful day's stag-hunting, when he decided to throw his hounds into Silk Wood, a famous covert that lies between Tetbury and Hawkesbury Upton. Almost immediately they gave tongue, and only a minute or two later out they went with a fine cry. But they were not on the line of a stag – their quarry was a fox. The ensuing hunt was so fast and so good that then and there the young Duke decided to devote his full attention to the pursuit of the fox. Acting on this impulse, he got rid of his stag-hounds. So it was through the whim of an eighteen-year-old two hundred years ago that fox-hunting became the pivot of life at Badminton.

My ancestor was not in fact breaking new ground, for in that subtle way that fashions tend to change with each ensuing generation, all the young blades in sporting circles were going fox-hunting, and in Grantham alone there were 294 horses stabled for the use of the smart set who wished to hunt with the nearby Leicestershire packs. That was round about the time that Hugo Meynell became Master of the Quorn. He was not only a country squire and a gentleman, but also a rich and educated man, well-known in both fashionable sporting circles and also in intellectual London ones, counting among his many friends the diarist, Dr Johnson. Youth were leading youth, and where they led, others followed. The eighteen-year-old Hugo Meynell brought in a new innovation by setting the times of his meet much later in the day than had hitherto been the custom, thus enabling many young men to travel more than fifty miles to hunt with him.

Indeed, up to the middle of the eighteenth century most packs of hounds hunted foxes when they could find them, but that was not often, for foxes were very scarce, every man's hand being against them. It is said that if a fox was seen, the news was given out from the pulpit of the Church, and the moment the service was over, out would rush the congregation all set to catch the varmint. It is fortunate for the survival of the fox as a species that the eighteenth-century Enclosure Acts came into being. The new fields with their hedges and ditches provided the young blades with jumps which whetted their appetite for more of the sport.

From about 1770 for some eighty years, the 5th, 6th and 7th Dukes of Beaufort not only hunted over their own country as it is now, but, owing to that shortage of foxes, they also took their hounds to hunt over what is now the Heythrop country in Oxfordshire. Until a year or so before the 7th Duke's death in 1853, there was a massive bi-monthly migration of hunt staff, horses and hounds to Oxfordshire, where they stayed for a month at a time, first at Cornbury and later at Heythrop House itself. Then they returned to Badminton again. It must have been an enormous undertaking, for even the housemaids went, and as this great exercise must always have taken place not only before there were any well-surfaced roads as we know them today, but mostly during the winter months, they necessarily had to contend with the worst conditions of snow, ice and mud, when the carriages no doubt slipped and slid hither and thither across very high land that was exposed to the full furies of the elements. Nor were the houses very comfortable when they reached them, for the 5th Duke's mother-in-law, Mrs Boscawen, was to complain that at Heythrop all the beds save for those in which she and her daughter slept were nothing but old velvet rags.

Even today, the livery of the Heythrop Hunt is almost identical to that worn by my own hunt servants, for they wear the particular shade of green that has always been worn by the outside servants at Badminton. In years gone by, those coats were always made of green plush, the material being specially woven for us and arriving in great bales. We had enough in stock to enable us to continue having the coats made for me and for my hunt servants for several years after the last war, but nowadays it is impossible to get stuff of that superb quality, and we have been obliged to fall back on ordinary worsted Melton. This has its credit side, all the same, for this material is reasonably waterproof, the rain tending to slide off it, not penetrating in anything like the same way as it did in the old plush. That stuff fairly sucked up the wet, and by the end of a really rainy day, our coats hung very heavily on our shoulders, not only tiring us, but adding enormously to the burden that our horses had to carry. We still use the original gold livery buttons, and these are carefully taken off an old coat to be sewn on to the new one. They are positioned down the back of the coat in exactly the same way as they were when it was usual for swords to be carried by those wearing livery, when the coat-tails had to be buttoned back.

This perpetual travelling from Badminton to Heythrop, and then from Heythrop back again throughout the hunting season must have presented some pretty problems to those whose business it was to make the elaborate arrangements necessary for each journey, causing a great upheaval all round. It certainly was not a way of life that would have suited me at all, for being a creature of habit, I could not bear the thought of spending four weeks at a time away from Badminton, as I have always liked to keep my finger on the pulse of things.

It must have been necessary to leave skeleton staffs at both ends in stables and in kennels so that the horses and hounds that were left behind would be fit and ready for work again the following month. During the cub-hunting season, it was the turn of the Badminton coverts in August, the Heythrop ones in September, with a return to Badminton again the following month.

What the people who lived around Badminton and hunted with our hounds thought of these bi-monthly migrations, I don't know, for it certainly must have done a lot of them out of sport, though many others followed hounds to Oxfordshire. They put up at hostelries all round the countryside, where they had frequent and extremely merry parties.

A group of people who positively welcomed the coming of the Badminton hounds was the sporting undergraduates at Oxford. They were only too glad to have the chance to put away their books, hire a horse and come out for a day's sport. Their behaviour in the Field was by no means exemplary, though, and they were shown up by my ancestor on one occasion after a wild young man had ridden so close to hounds as to press them right off the line.

Taking off his hat, the Duke said in a clear and icy voice: 'Sir, I have to thank you, and I beg every gentleman in the Field will follow my example and take off their hats to you, and thank you for spoiling a very good day's sport!'

When the 5th Duke got older he decided to emulate both his father and uncle, who between them had reshaped Badminton House. In 1783 he pulled down the existing church at Badminton and built another one a little farther to the east. He had this new and most attractive building joined to the main house by a long passage, the one we habitually use now when we go to services. Not only did he provide the family and the village with a new Church, but by so doing, he also provided a suitable picture gallery for all the ecclesiastical paintings that his uncle, the 3rd Duke had brought back with him from his Grand Tour sixty years earlier, and which had ever since languished in an attic. The 3rd Duke had also brought back some beautiful pieces of marble which his nephew now put to good use as a pavement, using some jasper and verde antico for the steps to the altar, with the Beaufort arms and their supporters partially inlaid with lapis lazuli. A memorial in the Church to the two brothers, the 3rd and 4th Dukes, depicts them seated in front of a map of the Estate, evidently planning all they were to do in the future – and, as we know, they carried those plans through to fruition.

Even though his father had provided a new Church for the family, the 5th Duke's younger son, Charles, did not make use of it. His marriage was the result of what his grandmother, Mrs Boscawen, described in her diaries (which were copious and full of interesting details), as 'an ill-advised expedition to Scotland' taken with Elizabeth Courtenay, the fourth daughter of Viscount Courtenay of Powderham, that gentleman having had no fewer than thirteen daughters. One summer evening in 1788, Elizabeth left her father's house in Grosvenor Square accompanied by her maid, and met Lord Charles at the end of Duke Street. He was waiting with a post-chaise to take them to Scotland where they were married. On their return, Charles left his bride at Heythrop, and journeyed on alone to Badminton to face the music. After this impulsive act when he was twenty, Lord Charles Somerset settled down, going into the Coldstream Guards where he reached the rank of Lieutenant-Colonel. When he came out of the army, he went into Parliament, and later on was appointed by the Prince Regent to the Governorship of the Cape of Good Hope. There he identified himself with the life of South Africa, and won the liking of the Dutch farmers by importing large numbers of horses, though his popularity was a little dimmed by his humanitarian views on slavery.

One of the most colourful characters in the history of our family came in the following generation. This was Lord Charles's nephew, my great-grandfather who was to become the 7th Duke.

As a very young man he was in the 10th Hussars, a regiment

described as 'a brilliant band of soldiers, sportsmen and dandies, who were known unofficially in society as "elegant extracts".' Many of the officers of that famous regiment distinguished themselves in a variety of ways – in war, sport and politics – and my great-grandfather was no exception. He was tall, handsome, dashing and dressed exceedingly well, so he was likely to be popular in a regiment with a reputation for daring and courage.

In his early youth he fell in love with the notorious Harriette Wilson, who caused a flutter in many eminently respectable dovecotes when she published her memoirs. Indeed it was the threat of their publication that made the Duke of Wellington write the time-famed words: 'Publish and be damned.'

Eventually young Henry Worcester, as he was then, fled from her arms, though not before he had taken her, riding side-saddle and dressed in Hussar uniform, with him on parade to inspect the troops.

He ran away from home in order to join the Duke of Wellington who was engaged in the Peninsular Wars. On hearing that he had gone, his father set off in hot pursuit, but was too late to stop him, as he reached the English Channel only to see the masts of his son's ship disappearing over the horizon on its way to the Bay of Biscay.

As so often happens with wild young men, wisdom came with years, and after having been an A.D.C. on the Duke of Wellington's staff at Waterloo, he returned home to settle down, becoming a Member of Parliament for Monmouth and marrying that same summer. He announced his engagement to Georgiana FitzRoy, a grand-daughter of the Earl of Southampton and niece of the Duke of Wellington, at a ball given by the Prince Regent at Carlton House; four days later she was given away in marriage by her uncle, the Iron Duke himself.

My ancestor was said never to look overdressed, but the outfit he wore when he took his bride to a ball given by the Duke of Wellington in Paris on their way back from their honeymoon defies belief, and sounds more like fancy dress to me. Over a white embroidered silk waistcoat with tight light-blue silk-web pantaloons, white silk stockings, and shoes described as 'brodés à jour', he wore a Beaufort Hunt evening coat of blue lined with buff and bearing the Beaufort Hunt Buttons. In those days they had GPR engraved on them, instead of the BH they now bear, those initials standing for George, Prince Regent, and they were intended as a compliment to 'the first gentleman of Europe'. To

15. *The hidden door leading to the Church. On the right of the portrait of Charles I is a letter in his own hand addressed to the Countess of Worcester.*

16. *The summer dining-room at Worcester Lodge,
scene of many happy parties. Designed by William
Kent, this lovely little building is situated at the end of
the three-mile-long avenue of trees stretching out to
the north of the house.*

17. The Front Hall, also designed and decorated by
Kent. Here, nearly 150 years later, my great-aunts
invented the game of Badminton. The five magnificent
equestrian paintings by Wootton were commissioned by
the 3rd Duke.

18. *Ajax, my Jack-Russell-type terrier, doesn't share my interest in the Hermit's Cell.*

19. *A group of servants posed for this photograph near the end of the last century, before I was born.*

crown all that sartorial extravagance, my great-grandfather wore a cocked hat!

On 3 May 1821, only seven short years later, his young wife, Georgiana, fell ill the morning after the King's Birthday Ball when they were staying with the Duke of Wellington at Apsley House. She was advised to have a cold bath, but far from doing any good, this drastic measure set up internal inflammation, and the poor girl, mother of two little daughters, said as she lay on her deathbed that she could not have believed it would be so painful to die.

It is no great surprise to learn that within the year my great-grandfather married again. This time his bride was Emily Culling-Smith who was the daughter of Charles Culling-Smith and his wife, the former Lady Anne FitzRoy. The surprise is that this new bride was his first wife's half-sister, as they shared the same mother. Perhaps that is why the couple had a very private ceremony at St George's, Hanover Square, and my great-grandfather's name appeared in the register as 'Henry Somerset, Widower'.

In 1835, when my grandfather, their first child, was eleven years old, an Act of Parliament was passed that was known as 'Lord Lyndhurst's Act'. Lord Lyndhurst was a close friend of my great-grandfather and his political leader; this Act provided that

> marriages between persons within the prohibited degrees of affinity which were solemnized before 31st August 1835 cannot be annulled for that cause; but such marriages (as well as those within the prohibited degrees of consanguinity [or blood-relationship]) solemnized since that date, are absolutely void and the issue consequently illegitimate.

For a man who evidently enjoyed life to the full, it is only natural that racing was one of the 7th Duke's favourite pastimes, and he did a great deal to improve British bloodstock.

He also took an active interest in the theatre, thoroughly enjoying amateur dramatics, and even appearing on the professional stage once or twice. He was severely criticised for doing this and incurred the displeasure of the Duke of York, but this did not daunt him. He was a founder member of the Garrick Club, and when Crockford's, the well-known gaming club was closed down owing to illegal practices, his immediate reaction was to set up one of its servants, a man called Pratt, in a club of his own, which is still known as Pratts, thus ensuring that there would be a suitable place in London for fashionable gaming.

He was also a great amateur whip, and a famous story is told of him when he was bringing a score of his friends home from the Brighton race-course. The road leading down from the course to the town is very steep, and in those days it had a greasy surface, so it was also very slippery. As the coach approached this slope, my great-grandfather was advised by a friend, who sat with him on the box, to put a skid on the wheel.

'Certainly not,' said my great-grandfather. 'That would probably cause the hind wheels to strike, and then we'd all turn over with such a heavy load. When I'm going down a steep hill I prefer my passengers not to know. If they are none the wiser, then they won't take fright.'

When he came out of the army, he joined the Gloucestershire Yeomanry, and, as his charger, he rode a beautiful milk-white mare full of Arab blood called Mayflower. A few years later he offered this lovely horse to Queen Victoria as a gift; but she was persuaded to refuse it by Sir Richard Quentin who declared that it was not a suitable mount for her – 'it is somewhat too spicy to be entrusted with so precious a burthen as our young and promising Queen.' Although I am sure that my great-grandfather would not have dreamt of offering the horse to Queen Victoria had he not thought it suitable – after all his eight daughters had had their early hunting training and experience on her back – a story told later by C. J. Apperley, who wrote under the name of 'Nimrod', may provide the reason for Sir Richard's doubts.

Nimrod was staying at Badminton for my grandfather's fifteenth birthday Meet, and the following morning he declared that he had never in his life ridden so fast to a Meet. 'You had better make a start,' he was advised by the head groom. 'The Duke is going to ride old Mayflower and he puts her along at a terrible pace.' Nimrod reported that they covered the seven miles in thirty-two minutes, and old Mayflower must have been at least twenty-three by that time. Perhaps it was as well that Queen Victoria had not accepted the gift.

Six years later this song was sung on the occasion of the coming of age of the Marquess of Worcester (my grandfather, the 8th Duke). The date was 1 February 1845.

Now rally round me, jovial friends, with merry
    hearts and free
A song in honour of the day we'll sing with
    social glee;
Fill high your flowing bumpers, boys and shout
    with three times three,
To Worcester Noble Marquis' health! and the majority
    Of this young English Nobleman, All of the
        Beaufort line,

For now, shall grateful hearts rejoice while
    mirth and pleasure reign,
And joy's full chorus shall resound through
    woodland hill, and plain
While *Badminton*'s proud halls shall loud
    re-echo round the strain,
Of welcome to the Noble Heir of its wide spread
    domain,
    This fine young English Nobleman, All of the
        Beaufort line

Far as the princely sway, from Severn's Banks to Wye
On every jocund breeze that blows, the joyful news
    shall fly:
Old Ragland shall repeat the theme, and Stoke's
    Manor reply:
While Troy shall be again besieged, but with
    a host who cry
    All Hail: to our young Nobleman, Pride of
        the Beaufort line
The horn of his Forefathers' may he its fame increase:
Sustain, like them the glories of his Plantagenet Race!
His bright ancestor's Coronet may he long live to grace
And still may history's faithful page long find an
    honourable place –
    For this fine young English Nobleman, All of
        the Beaufort line

In the middle of his sporting and political activities, my
great-grandfather, following in the family tradition of acquiring
property, bought a house in Arlington Street looking out on to
Green Park. He named it Beaufort House, and then proceeded

to gut it and have it completely renovated to the tune of a vast sum of money. Twelve years later, he sold it for £60,000; not only must he have recouped his outlay, but he must also have made a tidy profit into the bargain.

Eventually *anno domini* caught up with him as it does with us all, and he was obliged to stop riding. But that did not prevent him from following hounds, and he continued to go out in an open carriage drawn by a team of skewbald horses. My own father, who was only six years old when his grandfather died, told me that his first memory of seeing hounds was when seated in the hood of that carriage.

Such were the changing times that even then, back in the middle of the last century, the old Duke who had lived such a colourful and carefree life in the days of his youth, was full of foreboding about the future, and when he was dying he admonished his heir to bring up his son, my father, to earn his own living.

My grandfather was born in 1824, and died just before I was born, so he therefore lived through almost the whole of Queen Victoria's reign. As my family have always been Tories, they did not wield any political power during the last century, so military service for their country and local leadership in country sports and agricultural matters took precedence in their lives. My grandfather, like me, was a keen soldier, and also like me, was destined never to see active service. I am sure that he felt as deeply about that as I have always done.

He also had to watch the social changes that followed the first Reform Bill and the introduction of the railways that were to make so startling a change to the whole of the economic structure of this country during the last century, while being barred from taking part, owing to his political affiliations. I, too, have been thwarted in much the same way, as I have been unable to take a part even in the daily workings of the House of Lords, because I have held an office in the Royal Household, which has debarred me from giving any official intimation of my own political leanings. I suppose that I have, in effect, been disenfranchised, for as I am a Peer, I am unable to vote in General Elections, although I did in the four between 1921 and 1924, the year I succeeded. However, I can, and always do, put my cross on my ballot paper in local elections.

My grandfather's biographer spoke of him in glowing terms as being successful in all he undertook. Even making allowances for the rather sycophantic licence of a Victorian writer, I am sure there was a great deal of truth in what was said, for he evidently had the gift of a charming personality:

> ... The unfailing kindness of his heart, the fine courtesy of his manner, the unaffected desire to make those around him happy, marked him out as one who was to win the affection of his fellows for his good qualities and to obtain their forgiveness for his errors.

Those characteristics were also marked in my father, and I find a passage from Lodge's *Portraits* (Lodge being an almost exact contemporary of the 4th Earl of Worcester whom he is describing, and a writer of some distinction) most interesting:

> His familiar and easy nature was marked by infinite politeness and he led the chase, graced the ball and enlivened the Royal parties with equal ease and ability. In spite of his wealth and power, he made no enemies ...

My grandfather inherited a love of racing from his father, who took him when he was only six years old to watch a colt carry the Beaufort colours in to victory. When he succeeded to the title he registered new racing colours: blue with white hoops and a red velvet cap (the earlier ones having been a white jacket and blue cap). Those are the colours that I established; they are registered at Weatherby's and are used by my cousin and heir, David Somerset, for his racehorses.

My grandfather, having been introduced to racing so early in his life – indeed a story is told that once his pony ran away with him at Newmarket right past the winning post and through the town! – found it a lifelong interest. He bred all his own horses, keeping them at Allengrove (one of the names mentioned in Cromwell's Grant) and he had them trained by John Day at Danebury, where the Duke of Newcastle, the Earl of Westmorland and Lord Hastings also had their strings. In 1866 he won the One Thousand Guineas with Siberia, and his colt, Rustic, was a favourite for the Derby the year Lord Lyon won it. My grandfather never won that coveted classic, but his jockey, Fordham, carried the Beaufort colours to victory on Ceylon in the Grand

Prix, and on Vauban in the Two Thousand Guineas. He gave up racing for more than ten years after he had won the One Thousand Guineas for the second time with Scottish Queen. But he could not give it up for ever, and ten years later he won the Two Thousand Guineas for the second time with Petronel and the Caesarewitch with Ragimunde. He had his third win in the One Thousand Guineas with Rève D'Or, and she went on to win the Oaks, proving herself one of the best racehorses that my grandfather ever owned.

When he finally did give up racing, he went on breeding, took an active part as a member of the Jockey Club, and was one of the founders of the National Hunt Committee.

In his later years, when he was no longer able to take an active part in the hunting he had always loved so much, my grandfather, with the help of a writer called Alfred Watson, undertook the editing and a good deal of the writing of a series of books on sport called the Badminton Library. This Library covered subjects as diverse as hunting, driving, boating, yachting and golf. Between them, they turned out a series of twenty-eight meticulously researched books that were, and still are, extremely good reading. They are both authoritative and explicit on the subjects they cover.

My grandfather was most particular about detail and spent a good deal of time combing his own bookshelves for corroborative evidence of any particularly tricky point that arose. If he drew a blank, rather in the same way as he used to hunt his hounds, he would cast farther and farther afield, journeying to Bristol and even to London in search of the truth.

He expected his contributors to be real experts in their particular fields, not accepting, say, the membership of the Coaching and Four-in-Hand Clubs as being sufficient, or indeed any, qualification to contribute to the book on driving.

The very last volume of the series appeared a year before he died, entitled *The Poetry of Sport*. He had occupied himself with this project at a time of great personal tragedy, for his only daughter, Blanche, died of cancer. She had married the Marquess of Waterford who later had a hunting accident that left him a cripple for life. When he learned that his wife had inoperable cancer, the poor man committed suicide, which must have added to everyone's sorrow.

My grandfather, the 8th Duke, died 30 April 1899. Like all his forebears he was deeply mourned and greatly missed.

A Humble Tribute to His Grace
THE LATE DUKE OF BEAUFORT, K.G.

Alas! alas! for Badminton,
  All plunged in mournful grief,
They mourn the death of Beaufort,
  Their noble Duke and Chief.
No more, his kindly voice they'll hear.
  Well-known for miles around;
No more he'll hunt the county,
  With his noble pack of hounds.
And yet, it's scarce twelve months ago,
  When friends and tenants met
To present him with his portrait,
  It's a sight I'll ne'er forget.
Yes, I fancy I can see them,
  On that bright and sunny morn,
When they gave the Duke his portrait,
  On Badminton's fair lawn.
But now, alas, he's taken,
  And gone to his long rest,
And this I say, let none say nay,
  He was one of the best.
A good old English Gentleman,
  So kind and courteous too,
His like I'm sure 'twere hard to find,
  His equals very few.
And as for a good landlord,
  If we put it to the test,
We'll find that Beaufort really was
  One of the very best.
And wasn't he a sportsman once?
  One of the good old sort,
He always lent both purse and hand,
  To any kind of sport.
I'm sure the noble Worcester,
  Who takes his father's place,
Will keep up the traditions
  Of an ancient noble race.
And that, I am quite sure he will,
  And to the very letter,
And if he's like the rest of them,
  I'm sure we can't have better.

So now dear Beaufort, a last adieu,
  You've left this life's brief span,
A Gentleman, a Nobleman, a Soldier and a Man.

As I said, my grandfather's biographer spoke of him in glowing terms, and I am sure that from all I have heard about him, there was a good deal of truth in what was written. Of course, my grandfather died the year before I was born, but I well remember visiting my grandmother in the large castellated house that stood on a hill outside Bristol to which they had moved on my father's marriage.

In my grandfather's time, Society, as it was then called, was built on a very different structure than that of today – and more especially hunting society, which was a very close-knit affair that did not happily divide to allow newcomers to join its ranks. This is well-illustrated by the following story sent to me twenty-five years ago by Lieutenant-Colonel Montague Cooke of the Royal Horse Artillery, who was brought over as a small boy to Badminton by his uncle, Colonel Frank Henry (secretary to the Hunt for many years in the time of my grandfather), to enjoy a day's hunting.

Evidently Sir Hedworth and Lady Meux – though in his letter, Colonel Cooke preferred to leave the name a blank – had recently bought a large house and estate only a few miles from Badminton, where it was customary for hounds to meet once or twice a season. When he was arranging his Meets, my father, who was then still Lord Worcester, wrote a line to Lady Meux to inform her that they would be meeting on the lawn in front of her house.

Lady Meux, who was a charming woman and evidently a shrewd judge of character, had in her youth been a very lovely chorus girl at the Alhambra, and Society of the Nineties had not yet broken ranks and admitted actresses of the lighter stage. Consequently, Valerie Meux's neighbours, including my father, did not find favour with her and she therefore did not welcome a Meet of the hounds on her lawn, and she wrote and told my father so. However, he took no notice and the Meet was advertised to take place in the usual way.

From half-past ten onwards, the riders began to arrive, beautifully turned out in their Blue and Buff coats, buckskin breeches of the purest white, and shining boots with pale pink tops, mounted on superb blood horses, the ladies equally well attired, but of course wearing habits and riding side-saddle, with veils over their faces and nets over their immaculate hair. Just before a quarter-to-eleven, my father arrived in his green plush coat with his hounds and whippers-in, but there was no sign of either Sir Hedworth or of Lady Meux.

The Meet continued in its customary form, newcomers arriving, saying good morning to the Master, and then joining the rest of the throng, who were busily engaged in catching up with all the news and local gossip.

Colonel Cooke wrote:

> ... The hounds settled on the green lawn surrounded by this fashionable assembly. The day was favourable, scent would be good. The wintry sun gleamed through the elm woods on to green luscious grass. A true picture of Merrie England at her best.
>
> But the picture changes.
>
> Suddenly, without warning, there appeared from out of the wood our hostess, Lady Meux *seated on an elephant*!
>
> Her huge and massive steed lumbered forward straight for the lawn. Utter chaos reigned. Horses stampeded and bolted in all directions. Lords and ladies were thrown from their saddles. Glossy top hats, hunting whips and eye-glasses were strewn about the lawn. The hounds (bless them!) with a yelp and with no hesitation, fled in terror through the woods. Valerie Meux, with a merry twinkle in her eye, looked down from her elephant in triumph on to the ruins and scrummage below.
>
> This was *her* day.
>
> The gallant elephant, which she had hired from a travelling circus, had answered to the spur and enjoyed the fun and the shambles.
>
> It was not so long after this startling episode that Lady Meux's neighbours realised the true character of this sweet and very human woman, and took her to their hearts.

As well as being human, I would add that she was evidently very humorous as well. I am glad to say that my father was one of the first to see the joke, for he called on Lady Meux shortly afterwards, and they became firm friends.

Earlier still, Meets of our hounds were tremendous social occasions. We have a famous picture in the house of a Lawn Meet held at Badminton in 1845 which was painted by two brothers, William and Henry Barraud. My grandfather's biographer described the scene:

> ... The fixture for this day was The Lawn which implies Badminton Park House; and it generally happens that there are present, not only a numerous field of sportsmen, but carriages filled with ladies and gentlemen from Bath and Bristol, as also from the surrounding chateaus, merely to enjoy the spectacle ... Breakfast for at least fifty is served in the great hall with a full attendance of servants all in their evening costume, and a most agreeable mixture of *le dejeuner à la fourchette et à l'anglais* is presented to the choice of the company ...

This fork meal would probably have consisted of cold pheasants, cold ham and a choice of half a dozen other meats, followed by a pudding – fairly heavy provender with a day's hunting to follow.

For my eightieth birthday, one hundred and thirty-five years later, I also held a Lawn Meet outside Badminton, when there were some three thousand people on foot and several hundred mounted followers. It took the form of a joint Meet of my hounds with those of the Berkeley Hunt, and it was an extremely colourful occasion. The livery of the Berkeley Hunt is the yellow worn by the servants of the Berkeley family (yellow coats with green collars) and although it was April when we normally wear tweed jackets for hunting in the hill country, I asked everybody in my Hunt to come in their Blue and Buff, and my visitors to wear the livery of their own hunts; it was therefore a great spectacle of colour, for there were about fifty visiting Masters of Hounds all wearing their red coats. Everybody present was given a drink, but sad to say, hardly anybody returned their glass, keeping it as a souvenir of the occasion; so not only did I pay for the drink, but I footed the bill for the glasses as well!

Although I do not expect to have an entry in *The Guinness Book of Records*, I have in fact created a precedent in my own family, for no Duke of Beaufort up to now has lived as long, my father previously holding the record, as he was seventy-six when he died.

We have always had a family tradition of celebrating our birthdays in style, and when I was seventy, we had a supper at eleven o'clock at night at Swangrove House, a name mentioned in Cromwell's Grant, a pretty little early eighteenth-century house that was always intended as a dining-place for hunting and pleasure parties.

Verses written for my 70th birthday, 4 April 1970

The Birds and Beasts come out at night
To sing a merry glee,
The words were never in a book
But carved upon a tree

The tree, in spite of wind and storm
Stood firm and greater grew,
And so the letters deeply carved,
They grew much greater too.

These words we quote this Happy Night
With fear of no rebuke.
So all together loud and clear
We sing God Save the Duke

The Duke of Beaufort's Band
Oh! his name's the Duke of Beaufort
Who at Badminton does live,
And on his 70th birthday
A party he did give.
He asked his friends and neighbours
And formed a ducal band
And some of them were sober
But most of them were canned.

Chorus
Oh! the drums go bang and the cymbals bang
And the horns they blaze away,
Sir Peter pumps the old bassoon
The Duke the pipes does play.
Lord Harrison Allen he doodles the flute
And the horns they blaze away,
And the music is something grand

And a credit to his 70th year
Is the Duke of Beaufort's band.

Oh! his name is David Somerset
And from Bond Street he did come
To play in the Duke of Beaufort's band
And beat the big bass drum.
But of every hunting country
It's the bluest blooded band
And who is that who plays the harp?
... The Earl of Westmorland!
Oh! The music isn't perfect
It's sometimes rather rough,
But their uniforms atone for this
The famous blue and buff.
There is Molly and Peggy and Rona and Sally,
They lend a helping hand
By strumming on their four guitars
In the Duke of Beaufort's Band

Chorus
Oh! his name is Gerald Gundry
And he comes from Shipton Moyne,
He polished up his old trombone
And the band he came to join.
He puffs and blows for all he's worth
A noise to shatter glass!
Conducted by an army bloke
Called Colonel Hugh the Brass.
And there's Betty and Letty and Ronnie and Jane
They form a string quartet
They play in the Duke of Beaufort's band
The noblest ever yet.

Chorus
Now a most important person
Whose name you'll surely guess
She whistles as the others play
She is the Grande Duchesse
And here we all are gathered
In Swangrove's leafy nest

To greet the Duke, that grand gay Duke
And wish him all the best.

In the present climate of double entendre, I would prefer that last couplet to read: 'To greet the Duke, that sporting Duke – And wish him all the best.'!

Sir Peter – Sir Peter Farquhar; Lord Harrison Allen – David Harrison-Allen, who alas died a few years ago.
Molly – Then Lady Cranbourne, now Marchioness of Salisbury.
Peggy – Lady de L'Isle
Rona – Mrs Alec Scott
Sally – Sally, Duchess of Westminster
Hugh the Brass – Hugh Brassey, Chairman of the Hunt
Betty – Lady Farquhar
Letty – Lady Violet Vernon, who died a couple of years ago
Ronnie – Major Ronnie Dallas (Secretary of the Hunt).
Jane – The Countess of Westmorland

My parents habitually used the Front Hall as a sitting-room, and it was also put to another good use by a previous generation. One rainy day in the middle of the last century, my great-aunts were feeling rather bored, so they rigged up a string from the front door handle to the fireplace to try out the battledores and shuttlecocks that they had devised for themselves with both ingenuity and patience. They then proceeded to play a new game, making up the rules as they went along. At first, their aim was to keep the shuttlecock in the air for as long as possible, but the rules became more and more sophisticated as their skill grew, and eventually between them they had invented the game of Badminton. Nowadays there are world championships for the game, and in 1953 the reigning champions came to Badminton and played a demonstration game in our Front Hall, the measurements of which govern the required dimensions of a Badminton court.

The whole of Badminton House contains a labyrinth of corridors, little staircases and hidden corners into which the housemaids used to fade whenever they heard someone approaching, and which I found fascinating when I was a child. However, I was never brave enough to emulate my father's boyhood exploit, who, when he was about twelve years old, climbed out of a window on the west side of the nursery suite, and then proceeded to make his way round the entire face of the house, clinging on to the coping, and edging along inch by inch, until eventually his triumphant face appeared at one of the open windows of the suite of rooms that lies farthest away from the point where he began. However, what he had not realised before he started was that my grandparents were then occupying that suite of rooms, for they had a strange and nomadic habit of moving about the house, never staying in one place for more than a month or two at a time – rather in the way that the household had travelled between Badminton and Heythrop House in earlier years. The smile of triumph on my father's face was soon wiped off, for my grandfather did not hesitate to take immediate and suitable action, thus ensuring that his eldest son would never do such a foolhardy thing again.

This constant change and change-about of suites indulged in by my grandparents may have had its origins in their early way of life when my grandfather was in the Army. In one place they had only four rooms for themselves and two babies together with their nurses, so one corner of their sitting-room had to be screened off as a dressing-room. However, this proved no deterrent to their entertaining, and my grandmother engaged their guests in conversation to drown the sounds of her husband struggling to finish dressing behind the cover of that screen.

He evidently did not suffer what in me almost amounts to a persecution complex about punctuality. Brought up by my father on the strict principle that 'Punctuality is the politeness of princes.' I find that like George III, I am 'critically exact to time' almost to a point that if people are not early, I tend to think that they are late! That sounds very Irish, but stood me in good stead in all my dealings with King George V, who was also a great stickler for punctuality.

When my grandparents were stationed in Dublin, they had more accommodation, but it was much less convenient, for they had two small houses; as these houses were not adjoining, they had to keep running out of one and along the street to the other.

I myself have never found that I have been in the least tempted to emulate my father's roof-climbing exploits. Had I been at university it certainly wouldn't have been me who would have climbed the face of the college to place a domestic receptacle on the highest pinnacle, not because I feared the inevitable retribution that would follow such an act of bravado, but because I have never had anything of a head for heights. When I was in New York, I felt dizzy when I looked out of one of the high windows, and I can remember feeling distinctly queasy when I went to see them building the Severn Bridge and watched one of the men walking down one of those incredibly long curving girders. One of the things I am called upon to do each year in my role as High Steward of Bristol, and one that fills me with foreboding at the very prospect, is when I accompany the Lord Mayor of Bristol in his magnificent horse-drawn coach from the Mansion House in Clifton across to Ashton Park. I know that doesn't sound like an act of heroism, but believe me, as that coach sways and rattles along, so I become increasingly apprehensive at every wheel's turn, for I know full well that to reach Ashton Park, it is first necessary to cross Brunel's famous suspension bridge that spans Clifton Gorge at a dizzy height; it may be a masterpiece of design and engineering, but it is one that leaves me cold. As our vehicle turns to approach the bridge, I firmly fix my eyes on an immovable spot at the top of the wooded hills ahead, fervently praying that the Lord Mayor – and there is a new one each year – will not ask me to point out anything of interest either to left or to right, or, what would be even worse, down below, until we have safely reached the other side.

Strangely enough, my father told me that later in his life he too developed a fear of heights to such a degree that he could not believe that he had ever had the temerity to climb round the house the way he did in his youth.

My father was coming home from Eton at the end of one half when he was about fourteen, and he was to travel by stagecoach. Full of confidence in his own ability, he asked the coachman if he could take the reins.

As the diminutive figure sat on the box gathering those reins in his small hands, a fashionably dressed passenger strolled up and, giving a wink to the coachman, remarked that it was customary for gentlemen whips to smoke cigars, holding out his case. What else could my father do but accept the proffered Havana? Nor could he refuse to have it lit. However, on reaching his journey's end, he leapt down from the box where he had been seen to be getting paler and paler, and although he made a dash for the House, he did not reach it, and threw up on the gravel outside the front door.

My father has always been my hero, not only in hunting, but in every way. He was marvellous with hounds, and I am thankful that I was old enough to appreciate to the full the way in which he hunted them. He had a wonderful voice and used the horn superbly. He could trust his hounds absolutely not to change foxes – not like the ones we tend to have nowadays – though I must admit that I think that this in part was due to the better scenting conditions that existed in those days before the development of artificial fertilisers, and also before the internal combustion machine.

He did not ride hard in latter years, for as he grew older, he also got very heavy. Hounds would check and he would come up and ask the whipper-in where they had last hit the line. On being told, straight away my father would pick them up, but he would not go round to the right and round to the left like I used to do, covering a circle. No, he would take them straight on and immediately would hit the line of the fox.

He was a great man in many ways, and his deep and abiding interest in hunting lasted until the day of his death. The memory of his voice still rings in my ears, and I can hear again the wise advice that he used to give me, his only son.

His first season hunting hounds was in 1869 when he was twenty-two years of age, and as he went on until 1914, that means that he gave up at exactly the same time as me – at the age of sixty-seven.

The Huntsman In Green

A sportsman I'll give you, a gentleman born
   A man to be noted when seen:
The soul-stirring notes of his musical horn
Fall sweet to the ear and awaken the morn—
   Lord Worcester, the huntsman in green.

I've seen him on Beckford, the flea-bitten grey,
   A hunter both gallant and keen;
The old horse's spirit has drifted away,
But the rider remains, and is game to this day—
   Lord Worcester, the huntsman in green.

He is seen at his best on the side of a gale,
   He knows where his quarry has been
When the scent is both catchy and bad, and hounds
                               fail
To own it, he shows them each turn in the Vale,
   They trust him, this huntsman in green.

They've a character, too, have these beautiful hounds,
   Their necks are both graceful and lean;
How handy they seem, ever kept within bounds,
From the heart of the wood their sweet music
                             resounds,
   And the cheer of their huntsman in green.

20. *The 5th Duke, who inherited the title when he was only twelve, painted by Reynolds when he was at Oxford. It was this ancestor who introduced fox-hunting to Badminton.*

21. Painting of the 6th Duke with his younger brother, Lord Charles Somerset, by the Park Pond. A groom holds the pony.

22. Painting of Vauban, one of a group of paintings of 'classic winners' which hangs in the passage of the house. In 1876 Vauban won the Two Thousand Guineas and the Prince of Wales Stakes.

23. *My great-grandfather, the 7th Duke, one of the
most colourful characters in the family.*

24. *A magnificent lifesize portrait of my grandfather and grandmother by Sir Francis Grant. He is mounted on a dapple grey with two of his favourite hounds, and she is on the Andalusian mare that had won so many races, which he had bought for her when they wintered in Gibraltar.*

There's a whistle away, and a cap in the air,
    But never a fuss or a scene:
The Blue and Buff squadron intend to be *there*,—
Those men who can ride and those ladies so fair,
    Who follow the huntsman in green.
And over the open they race and they ride,
    Till the fox by the hedgerow is seen;
The huntsman's big hunter makes use of his stride,
And those who are leading the galloping tide,
    Hear 'Who-oop!' from the huntsman in green.

The crowd has gone home, and Lord Worcester is still
    As keen as a lad of fourteen;
See, the sunlight is dim on the opposite hill,
But he walks a good fox to his death with a will,
    He's a huntsman, this huntsman in green.

When home is the word, there's a smile on his face,
    It tells of contentment, I ween:
He has shown us a gallop and handled a brace,
But it's what we expect, and it's often the case,
    With the Badminton Huntsman in green.

Sess, sess, brother sportsman, go home and lie down
    Take your soup and clear out the tureen:
Sess, sess, brother sportsman, go home and lie down.
Long, long may you lead us in chase with renown,
    Still known as the huntsman in green!

(W. Philpotts Williams, *Baily's Magazine* Dec. 1896.)

When my parents were using the front hall as a sitting-room
we grew accustomed to using what we call 'the step door' on the
west side of the house. That has become the entrance that we
habitually use to come in and out of the house, and as it has a
portico, visitors are able to alight from their vehicles and enter
the house without getting wet.

Set high up in the wall outside is a circular iron frame (and this
was *not* used by any aunts of mine to invent net-ball!), which
held a flare that used to light up the entrance, giving out a
welcoming and reassuring blaze of light when we returned after
dark from parties in the Christmas holidays.

Of course, in the days of my childhood, the whole house was

lit by oil lamps and candles (we never had gas, for it would have had to be piped from Bath or Bristol, and that would have been much too far), which may sound very romantic and did look lovely, but in practice it caused an immense amount of work. A special lampman had to be employed whose sole duty was to trim and light all the lamps and replenish the candles before they burnt out in both the house and the kennels.

As for the heating of so large a house, dozens of people were concerned not only with the provision and shifting of the fuel, wood and coal, but with the kindling and lighting of all the fires and their constant re-stoking. It was difficult enough to keep the body of the house warm, but masses of hot water also had to be provided each day, and the kitchen ranges had to be kept at a constant temperature for the vast amount of cooking carried out all the time. We even had our own chimneysweep, and, what is more, we had our own fire-engine. That ancient machine, sole survivor of all our old wheeled vehicles, all the others having been destroyed in the Blitz when they were in a museum in Bristol, is still to be seen by the general public in the museum that is now incorporated in the University of Bristol's buildings. When we have any of the Royal Family staying in the house, we are required to have a fire-engine, but a modern one, stationed permanently by the pond outside the step door.

That puts me in mind of a funny incident that happened to me when I was staying at Windsor for the Ascot Races one year. Also in the party was a foreign king who spoke very little English. Wanting to speak to one of his friends, he picked up a telephone that he found in the corridor outside the door. To his dismay, that innocent action caused all the fire alarms to sound, and the whole castle was encircled by fire-engines and helmetted firemen, for it was in fact a red telephone, which is only used to report a fire.

Electricity was installed in most of Badminton in 1922 just before I married, and although it must have cost a lot to put in, it certainly served to cut down on labour. However, when there was a question of converting the French candelabra in the ball room which also doubles as our drawing-room, the ladies rebelled. The very idea of glaring electric light there filled them with horror, and they declared that the candles must stay, as the light thrown by them was far more flattering to the female complexion.

However, eventually we were persuaded to move with the times, and those lovely eighteenth-century French chandeliers were converted to electricity in 1936. Only a few years ago we made the horrifying discovery when some other work was being done, that the chandeliers, each enormously heavy, were held up to the ceiling by only the most slender of supports, and could have come crashing down at any moment.

Although our House is big, it is and always has been essentially a home, and we occupy most of it with our dogs and birds, showing it to the public every Wednesday afternoon during the summer months, and often lending it to organisations who want to have dances or fashion shows or concerts in aid of one charity or another.

My wife has always shared my devotion to the House, and it gives her the greatest pleasure to show it to the visitors who flock in from far and wide, herself. I think that many of them are surprised when they discover that the person showing them around, who seems to be so knowledgeable, is in fact the Duchess. But what more natural than that the owner's wife should wish to be the one to show her own home to visitors. What we have we have always been happy to share, and I am glad that people enjoy walking in the Park and fishing in the Park Pond. All I ask is that they stick to a very simple set of rules and show consideration to others – and, above all, take their rubbish home with them!

11 November

Tally-Ho!

Sir, – I am alarmed to learn from your leading article today that the Duke of Beaufort rides in a car bearing the registration number MFH 1

At these works we travel in FOX 1. May I be assured that, should we happen to meet his Grace on the road, no unseemly incident will occur?

Yours faithfully,
H. P. Forder

Samuel Fox & Son, Ltd.,
   Stocksbridge Works,
   Sheffield,

My reply to that was as follows:

Tally-Ho!

Sir, – With reference to Mr. H. P. Forder's letter of November 11, will you please assure Mr. Forder that his car FOX 1 need have no fear of meeting my car MFH 1, as there is no possibility of my visiting the Sheffield district before the start of the cricket season, when Fox-hunting is over.

Yours faithfully,
Beaufort

Badminton, Glos.

(letter page, The Times)

CHAPTER SIX

HUNTING: A WAY OF LIFE

Not for the lust of killing, not for
  the place of pride,
Not for the hate of the hunted we
  English saddle and ride,
But because in the gift of our fathers
  the blood in our veins that flows
Must answer for ever and ever the
  challenge of 'Yonder he goes!'

(W. H. Ogilvie)

Although I fully realise that by sheer virtue of my position in the hierarchy of this country, I was born to a life of privilege, I feel very strongly in that I was also privileged to be born to a country life, and was not obliged to earn my living in London or some other city, in spite of my great-grandfather's gloomy prognostications and advice to his son on his deathbed. I earnestly believe that it is only people who have been brought up in the country who can appreciate to the full all the activities that are part and parcel of the country way of life, and this includes not only farming, but also sporting pursuits – and so field sports come into this category.

Obviously the hunting of the fox is my chief concern, as it is to that particular field sport that I have devoted a large part of my life. I have been a Master of Foxhounds for more than fifty years – nearer sixty – so I reckon that I ought to know more about fox-hunting than most other people.

All the terms used in the hunting field come as second nature to hunting people, but I quite see that to those who have not enjoyed the benefit of a country upbringing, even the title of huntsman may be difficult to comprehend, for to the outsider it might surely seem that all people who hunt are themselves huntsmen. That is not so. For the benefit of my readers who may find themselves a little confused by all the elaborate phraseology that we foxhunters take for granted, I will try not only to explain the structure of the hunt but also the names and functions of the people who take part in it.

During the two centuries that fox-hunting has been a popular sport in the British Isles, divisions have been made in the land, and these divisions are hunted exclusively by certain packs of hounds, each pack having a name of its own and being called 'a Hunt'. Although many of these names such as the Quorn, the Fernie, the Heythrop, the Meynell, The College Valley, the Ledbury, and my own which is known as the Duke of Beaufort's Foxhounds, to take but a handful, do not immediately tell the uninitiated where they are to be found, to those in the know the names are self-explanatory. Indeed, when a stranger comes out with a pack of hounds, the question 'Where do you come from?' is not answered by, say, Northamptonshire, but by the name of the pack of hounds with which they hunt, or in whose country they live. In the case of Northamptonshire it may be any one of the following: the Pytchley, the Woodland Pytchley, the Grafton, the Oakley, or the Bicester and Warden Hill. Many of the names describe the district, but many more are the names of the people who originally founded that particular pack of hounds.

The ground over which each pack hunts is called their 'country', and the boundaries are very clearly defined, and an accurate record is kept of them by the Master of Foxhounds Association, an arbitrary body that was founded in the 1880s and had its origins in an unofficial body that operated from Boodles Club in St James's, London, under the leadership of my grandfather.

The administration of a Hunt is usually conducted by a Committee with the usual officers, such as Chairman, Secretary, Treasurer, etc., and the members are mostly either local landowners or hunting farmers, with a sprinkling of other people who are willing to devote the necessary time to helping with the running of the Hunt. The actual hunting is under the leadership of a Master, or nowadays more probably two or three Joint Masters, this being a common practice now when things are so expensive that it is necessary to spread the load. The hunt staff are employed by them, and not by the Committee. No man can serve two masters – however paradoxical that may seem after what I have just said about Joint Masters. What I mean, of course, is that there must be an ultimate authority, and as far as the hunt staff are concerned, that rests in the Masters. In practice it is usual for each Joint Master to specialise in a certain aspect of the hunt; one of them perhaps dealing with matters relating to the staff, another with the actual hunting, and maybe a third with the kennels and hound-breeding programme.

The hunt staff are generally made up of a huntsman and one or two whippers-in with some kennel men to look after the hounds at the kennels, and a stud-groom with strappers working under him to care for the horses.

The huntsman's duties are to know and discipline his hounds so that he can take them out to find a fox. Having found one he lays the pack on to that particular fox's scent, and they will then pursue and eventually kill that fox. Put like that, it sounds as simple as pie, but believe me, it is not! However, this is not intended as a treatise on hunting – you must go elsewhere for that – and I am not going to go into details. All I want to provide here is an outline of the general set-up for those who do not already know it.

The object of the whole exercise is embodied in the words '. . . to find a fox. Having found one they will pursue and eventually kill that fox'; the words should be added, 'in an organised and disciplined manner'. The reasons for this are two-fold. One is that if the fox population is not controlled in this way, severe losses will be caused by foxes to farmers by taking lambs, to poultry-keepers by raiding the chicken runs, and to game-preservers by taking their birds. The other reason, and one that is even more important from a humane point of view, is that if, as I said before, the Hunt does not do the job efficiently and properly, it is only natural that some farmers will take the law into their own hands (and who could blame them?); their methods are rarely either sporting or humane, very often being downright cruel, for there is seldom any differentiation made between a dog-fox and a vixen that may well be suckling her young. If such a vixen is killed, then her litter will starve to death. I am not going to make an Aunt Sally of myself by saying that hunting is never cruel, for that would obviously not be true, but it is normally conducted under a code of rules that are strictly adhered to by conscientious Masters of Hounds – and believe me, they would not last long as M.F.H.'s in a fox-hunting country if they did not stick to the rules that are clearly laid out and defined by the Master of Foxhounds Association.

Sometimes a Master will prefer to hunt his own hounds, and there are many of these amateur huntsmen. In that case, he will employ a man who is known as Kennel Huntsman, who hunts hounds when the Master is unable to do so himself. I myself hunted my own hounds for forty-seven seasons, exactly the same length of time as my father before me.

A whipper-in is not there to whip the hounds, but his duty is to help the huntsman by keeping the hounds together; should they divide on two foxes, then it is he who has to go and fetch one lot and bring them back to the main body of the pack, and he also has to pick up stragglers. He has many other duties, of course, but I think it would be true to say that his main function in life is to help the huntsman to maintain hound discipline in the field, and to help with the general care of the hounds in kennels.

Now we come to the word 'field'; this has two functions in hunting terminology. When it is used in the context of the previous paragraph, it means during the course of hunting a fox. But the same word is also used to describe the people who come out to enjoy a day's hunting mounted on a horse – and they, as a body, are known collectively as 'the Field'. Confusing, isn't it?

As I said before, to those born and bred to it, such terms are second nature, and it is when I come to try to explain them I realise to the full how difficult it must be for the layman to understand it all fully and completely, without having actively participated in the sport himself.

In order to be able to hunt, obviously a great deal of money is required, and this necessitates each mounted member of the Field paying either an annual subscription or a payment for the day on which they come out, which is called a 'cap'. This expression came to be used I expect when people used to be asked to put a donation into a cap, just as people used to be given Christmas tips in a box, hence the terms 'Christmas box' and 'Boxing Day . Obviously more money than that needs to be raised, so each Master is required to put up a certain amount himself, either in cash or kind, each season, and most Hunts nowadays have active Supporters' Clubs that arrange all manner of entertainments to raise money for their Hunt.

Without the goodwill of the local farmers, there would be – could be – no hunting at all, and that is why when one of my own farms comes in hand, and I am looking for a new tenant, I choose him very carefully, always trying to find someone who either hunts himself or at any rate is pro-hunting, as well as being a man who will farm the land well. It stands to reason that we fox-hunters owe a great debt of gratitude to the farmer, for even though we do a specific job for them by ridding the country of an over-population of foxes, to do so we gallop over their land inevitably sometimes causing damage. It must always be remembered that we do this by invitation only, and certainly not by right.

You will see from all this that hunting is largely a matter of teamwork, but you must not run away with the idea that hunting is all pleasure, because that is not so. It is a dedicated way of life, and once it has been embarked upon, like any other vocation, it is virtually impossible to give up. Believe me, it is not pleasant getting up at five o'clock every morning for a couple of months or so in the autumn which is the time we go cub-hunting, when the young hounds get an opportunity to learn what it's all about, and so do the foxes.

It is not any fun, either, being compelled to go out, and once out to stay out in all weathers, regardless of one's state of health, pounding on up hill and down dale in filthy, blinding rain that has more than a touch of ice in it, and visibility down to a matter of yards, with hounds away in front of you and you know not quite where.

Why, you will ask, do people go out hunting day after day if it's like that? Well, it is very simple really. There is a disease that is extremely contagious, which once caught, tends to become chronic. That disease is called 'fox-hunting'. Fox-hunting holds a sort of magic that once experienced can never be forgotten. It becomes almost like a drug for it is certainly an addiction, and, like falling in love, it is inexplicable. In the same way as poets and writers have tried to explain love, so too they have written about hunting, and very successfully.

> Stags in the forest lie, hares in the vally-o!
> Web-footed otters are spear'd in the lochs;
> Beasts of the chase that are not worth a Tally-ho!
>   All are surpass'd by the gorse-cover fox!
>   Fishing, though pleasant,
>   I sing not at present,
>   Nor shooting the pheasant,
>   Nor fighting of cocks;
>   Song shall declare a way
>   How to drive care away,

Pain and despair away,
Hunting the fox!
(R. E. Egerton–Warburton 1880.)

Here is a description of a hunt over two hundred years ago which tells a tale in very few words:

November 19, 1776:
From Lyde Green Head, Bristol two rings in the Vale (15 miles), then to the hills, first to Sir William Codrington's woods at Doddington, then to the Duke's woods at Didmarton, Hawkesbury Upton, Kilcot, and killed between Kilcot and Frocester. Found at 7.30 and killed at 4.00. All the Field were thrown out and 6 people out of 17 (hounds) in at the death. They were found lying on their bellies with Reynard in their midst. Estimated distance, 50 miles, and the largest fox seen in these parts.

Perhaps the most historic day of all in the history of our Hunt, certainly the most famous, was that of the Greatwood Run, which took place thirty years before I was born.

The Meet was at Swallets Gate on Wednesday, 22 February 1871, when my father, then a twenty-three-year old subaltern in the Blues, was hunting 17½ couple of hounds mounted on a horse called Beckford, a fleabitten grey. It was Ash Wednesday, and on the way to the Meet my father gave the order that the customary blast on the coach horn must not be blown as they approached the villages, as it was the first day of Lent. Having given that order, he forgot all about it, his mind being on the day's sport that lay ahead.

The fox was found at the east end of Grittenham Great Wood after a long draw. The wind had changed to the south-west, and very few people heard the whistle as the fox went away, standing where they were on the edge of the covert. So only my father and his First Whipper-in, Heber Long, and comparatively few of the Field were with hounds as they settled down to run uphill in deep country. However, the fox was headed and swung round again towards the wood. He was a bold fox, and was obviously determined to make his point, so, entering the wood on the opposite side to that from which he had originally left it, he went straight through without hesitation. The wonderful cry of hounds as they followed him through the covert enabled the rest of the Field to come on terms, and they had, in fact, been saved three miles of very stiff going.

The fox then headed towards Brinkworth Brook, and managed to get across. Not so with the Field. A few of the more dashing young riders charged it and got over, but many more found their horses refusing, and many more still had a ducking. My father, who had been lucky enough to pick up his second horse, Williamstrip, as he crossed the Brinkworth road, and a few others who were in front saved their horses a little by going over the bridge. When hounds reached the village of Brinkworth, they found themselves at a loss. However, my father gave them time to cast themselves, and while they did so, he watched them closely. Suddenly his sharp eye saw one of his most trustworthy hounds show unmistakable signs of renewed interest, so with a low whistle, he cast them on, and was rewarded by seeing them settle on the line again, and they ran hard for Somerford Common. Here they never paused or wavered, and it was evident that the fox had gone right through that famous V.W.H. covert.

Perhaps because he felt that hounds were too close to him, or maybe because he had met some obstacle, the fox started to twist when he left the covert, but hounds were not misled, and were never off the line, and from then on their fox skirted all the other coverts where he might have found shelter. Possibly that is because hounds were pressing him too hard.

They ran hard over the Tadpole Vale, and those members of the Field who were still there found their horses, not unnaturally, tiring and beginning to flounder and fumble at their fences. This was when it became necessary to save the horses as much as possible, for there was obviously not a hope of the second ones being brought up.

Cricklade was left behind, and the River Thames lay in front. In my father plunged where he saw a cattle drinking-place on the opposite bank that would offer him a way out, swam the river and scrambled out of the water right on the heels of the tail hounds, though the leading ones were well away in front. By that time they were running mute, which is not surprising. Fortunately the line of the scent ran parallel to the canal, so my father was able to save his gallant horse a little by taking it along the tow path.

Once again the Thames had to be crossed, the wiser people using the bridge at Castle Eaton. A couple of eager followers tried to swim the river again, and were very nearly drowned for their pains.

By this time, hounds as well as horses were wearying, but their good condition and fitness told, and on they went, though luckily the pace was slow, for as two hounds called Hannibal and Nathan led the pack through some gardens and a farmyard, my father was obliged to abandon his horse that by then was absolutely done for, and follow his hounds on foot, accompanied by two of the only remaining members of the Field, Dr Alfred Grace, who often played cricket for the Badminton team – though his more famous father, W. G. Grace never would – and a Captain Candy. Fortunately a local farmer, Mr Hynam, quickly summed up the situation and went swiftly into action, clapping a saddle on the back of a good stout cob, which he then rushed up to my father, who mounted it and breathlessly came up to find hounds marking their fox to ground in a drain under the vicarage garden at Highworth in the Old Berkshire country, a sixteen-mile point, though it was of course very many miles farther as hounds ran.

He was met by a furiously indignant clergyman, not so much put out by the invasion of his garden, but by the fact that they were hunting at all on Ash Wednesday. That was the last thing that my father had been thinking about as he had driven his horse on in what had turned out to be a three-and-a-half-hour hunt, during which he had had to swim the River Thames twice, and then continue on a horse that was failing more and more with each fence that had to be cleared.

However, bringing all his charm to bear, my father managed to smooth down the angry clergyman's ruffled feelings, and it was a very weary set of horsemen – Colonels Ewert and Dickson, Messrs Tom Wild and Pitman (it was Mr Pitman who had led my father's horse when he was obliged to take to his feet), Captain Candy, Mr Byng and Dr Grace all did the whole run, while Mr Jenkins had joined in after the first round and was there at the end; my grandfather arrived about a quarter of an hour later with Lord Arthur and Mr Granville Somerset. All of them turned their weary horses' heads towards Swindon where they found a special train waiting for them that took them back as far as Chippenham, which was the nearest they could get to Badminton in those days before the railway had been built that ran near to the house.

But my father did not accompany them on to that train. It seems hardly credible after such a hunt, but he caught the next one that was travelling in the opposite direction, and a couple of hours later, mudstained and weary, he arrived back at Albany Street just in time to bath, change and lead his troop to the Horse Guards to inspect the barracks, it being his turn to act as Orderly Officer that day!

My father was a truly wonderful man.

> How they drive to the front! – how they bustle and spread,
>> Those badger-pied beauties that open the ball!
> Ere we've gone for a mile, they are furlongs ahead,
>> As they pour like a torrent o'er upland and wall.
> There is raking of rowel and shaking of rein
>> (Few hunters can live at the Badminton pace),
> And the pride of the stable's extended in vain,
>> And the Blues and the Buffs are all over the place.

> (A poem written by Whyte Melville for my father, after a good day near Tetbury, where Whyte Melville lived)

I think I must include a description of the best hunt I ever enjoyed. There was a large Field out on Saturday, 29 December 1928, when my hounds met at Rodbourne. It was a dull, rather mild day, with a south-westerly wind, but there had been very heavy rain right through the night before, and so the ditches were bank high, and many a horse and rider came to grief in consequence.

Before I left the house to ride on to the Meet, I had had a look at the glass, and was delighted to find that it was rising, and all the signs were that it was going to be perfect hunting weather for my twenty and a half couple of bitches.

We found our fox in Bincombe Wood, and my Second Whipper-in holloaed him away before hounds spoke in covert. They got away well together, and then hunted nicely to Seagry Wood. I fully expected as had happened so often before, that our fox would then go to Draycot Park, and then there would be a subsequent long spell of woodland hunting with all its attendant frustrations and delays.

However, today was different, and our hunted fox was evidently different too, for he ran straight down the main ride, turned out to the left past Seagry House, and then went away over a strongly fenced country towards the flooded banks of the

River Avon. As hounds ran across one of the fields, a carthorse colt took fright, and galloping through the pack, knocked poor Woodbine, winner of many prizes at Peterborough, unconscious. Fortunately the Second Whipper-in was able to carry her to a nearby farmhouse, but that meant that I had to do without his services for the rest of the hunt, for he never managed to catch up with us until we had killed.

The flooded water meadows slowed hounds up, but I could see that our fox had obviously headed for the road-bridge near Dauntsey House. There was a party of men working on the bridge so the fox was prevented from crossing, and he waited in a small spinney by the side of the bridge until hounds were almost on him. Then at the very last moment, up he jumped, and by then he had almost left it too late, so he had no choice but to race right through the working party, as he made a dash across the bridge.

As he sped on across Dauntsey Park, so hounds got a view of him, and off they went like bats out of hell over the Dauntsey Vale, which from the riding point of view was the best part of the whole hunt. Passing close to Miss Iles's covert, leaving Greatwood, famous of course for that other hunt I have just described, to their left, on they tore, crossing both the railway and the canal and heading straight for the reservoir below Hillocks Wood. This stretch of water is about half a mile long and more than a hundred yards wide, but hounds went straight for the middle, checking in the withybed that lies on its northern bank. Swinging back into the fields, they cast themselves to the right and then to the left, but they could not hit off the line, until suddenly Candid, a wonderful fourth-season bitch, spoke and immediately plunged straight into the reservoir and swam across. The moment I saw her launch herself into the water I swiftly went into action, racing up to pick up the pack so that I could gallop them round to meet her as she landed on the far side.

Immediately striking the line, away they went. Fortune was certainly with us that day, for quite by chance, the local earth-stopper was working in Hillock's wood where there is a huge badger-earth. On hearing the cry of the hounds coming towards him, he rushed to the earth and was just in time to head the fox and thus prevent it from going to ground.

Thwarted in that way, on it went past Tockenham Wick, through Vastern, re-crossed the canal and ran over both branches of the railway line between which the Brinkworth Brook twists and turns forming the boundary between my hunt and that of the V.W.H. (Cricklade) as it was in those days, before the two V.W.H. countries amalgamated.

There is a ford near to where hounds crossed, but after all the rain during the previous night, that water was as bank-high as we had found all the ditches. Even so, there was nothing for it but to plunge in, which I did, followed closely by my First Whipper-in, and somehow we managed to get across and then to scramble out on the other side. We were followed by about a dozen of the Field, including four ladies. Of those four, two were sisters and very well known for their skill and daring in the hunting field, another was the wife of a neighbouring Master, and the fourth had been 'a good 'un to follow, a rum 'un to beat' since before the Great War – and often on the worst of horses.

Hounds hunted steadily on, skirting Wootton Bassett on their right. As I galloped by, it seemed as if the whole population of the town was gathered on the hill that lies above the allotments, and when they viewed our fox, they gave a holloa that would have rivalled the Yorkshire roar when the favourite gets home in the Leger. Neither fox nor hounds took a jot of notice, but on they ran, leaving Coped Hall on their left as they crossed the Swindon Road.

There, hounds were checked by some cattle, but it was only a moment or two before Wagtail by Berkeley Waggoner, picked up the line again, and away they went, driving on even harder than before.

> Ah! don't they mean mischief, the mercilous ladies,
> What fox can escape such implacable foes!

On they went, leaving a series of beaten horses behind them and, just like in the Greatwood Run, there was no question of any second horsemen managing to get to us. On we had to struggle over deep and hairy country, with Spittleborough Farm close on our right hand. But suddenly there in front of us, in the middle of a large grass field we could see hounds breaking up that fox which they had hunted so truly and so well for two and a quarter hours, with a point of eleven and a half miles, and every hound – except of course poor Woodbine who had been kicked by the young carthorse right at the beginning of the hunt – on at the finish. I imagine that that truly gallant fox was making for Lydiard Park, which lies about half a mile farther on.

The things that are essential for a great hunt are a good fox –

that goes without saying – and a good pack of hounds, with a lot of good luck thrown in for good measure. There is no doubt that on that day in late December 1928, we were blessed with all three.

'Hard luck' stories are the usual and expected sequel to all good hunts, and that day was no exception, but fortunately the going was so soft that even though there were a good many spills, nobody was badly hurt.

Poor Tom Newman, my Kennel Huntsman, who had given me and my sisters so much pleasure with his yarns when we were children, had arranged to ride out from the kennels to meet hounds at the first draw. Arriving a few minutes late, he found himself getting farther and farther behind as he tried in vain to catch up, and eventually he was obliged to return home, having ridden nearly forty miles without ever seeing a hound.

It is interesting to relate that during the following season, 1929–30, we enjoyed two splendid hunts from Bincombe across the Dauntsey Vale, one of them to Greatwood and the other to Lyneham Banks. In my heart of hearts I hope and believe that on each of those occasions we were hunting foxes that were following in the footsteps – or perhaps it should be pads? – of their sire which without hesitation I would describe as the stoutest fox I ever hunted.

The Hunting 'IF'

If you can hunt, and stay among the leaders
And yet not thrust nor over-ride the Hounds,
If you can take a dozen nasty 'headers'
Yet never let your temper out of bounds.

If at the Meet some inexperienced fellow
Backs into you, and trouble is astir,
If you can merely smile, and do not bellow
'Damnation! Where is your red ribbon sir?'

If you can see that chap you've always hated
Sent flying in the mud by playful buck,
And do not laugh aloud, nor feel elated,
But stop and help him up and say 'Hard Luck!'

Or if the girl you loathe is the aggressor,
'butts in' and leaves you lying in the ditch,
If you can say 'That girl rides well God bless her!'
Instead of calling her a Naughty 'Witch'!!

25. *A painting by the Barraud brothers of the Lawn Meet of 1845. My great-grandmother is arm-in-arm with Mary's great-grandfather, the Duke of Cambridge.*

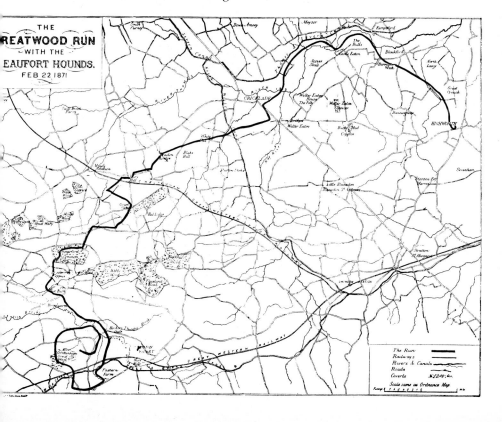

THE
REATWOOD RUN
WITH THE
EAUFORT HOUNDS.
FEB 22 1871

27. *I have devoted a large part of my life to foxhunting.*

If you should feel at times your nerve is breaking,
Yet take yourself in hand e're 'tis too late
And jump the monstrous fence that sets you quaking
Nor look with longing eyes at gap or gate.

If when you feel your horse is blown and jaded
Just near the finish of a glorious Run
You can leave off, with thought of Self all faded,
And pat his heaving flanks and say 'Well done!'

And if, when as the shades of night are falling
You're jogging homewards with a well earned thirst,
And, though a steaming bath and drink are calling,
You see your mount is fed and watered first.

If when at last before the fire, contented,
While telling others all about the ride
You leave that bank the height that Nature meant it,
Nor let that four foot ditch grown twelve feet wide!!

If you are always loyal to your Master
And never brag about the things you'd do,
Then, in the face of any dire disaster
You'll be a Sportsman, and a Marvel too!

(Angela Shortt)

CHAPTER SEVEN

MASTER OF THE HORSE

... The Lord Chamberlain and the Lord Steward are senior to the Master of the Horse on all occasions except when the Queen is mounted or in a horse-drawn carriage. On the latter occasions, the Master of the Horse is senior to all on parade and has the right to ride next to the Queen. He is responsible for Her Majesty's safety on all State and formal occasions whenever Her Majesty is mounted or in a carriage, and for the smartness and turnout of men, carriages and horses on all such occasions.

When King Edward VIII came to the throne for his short and ill-fated reign, one of the first things he did was to ask me to become his Master of the Horse. Naturally I was both thrilled and honoured by his invitation, the more so as our family connections with the office of Master of the Horse go right back in the history of our family, for it first came into being during the life-time of the founder of our family, the Plantagenet, John of Gaunt, Duke of Lancaster. Up to then, the man who had carried out the duties was known as 'Keeper of the Horse'.

In the 9th century, King Alfred had what were known as 'horse-thegns', men of noble birth who embodied the knightly virtues long before the French introduced the practice of chivalry as a positive art into Europe in the Middle Ages. Nowadays those qualities of chivalry seem to be curiously out-of-date with all the talk there is of equality of the sexes; but in mediaeval times, the ideal characteristics of a knight included not only devotion to the service of women, but a practical defence of their persons and of their honour. King Alfred naturally chose his horse thegns from among those men who were his closest friends – in other words, he chose men he could trust. From that time until now, whenever the appointment of Master of the Horse has been in the Monarch's gift, with no political strings attached, the men chosen for the office have generally been those who both share the sovereign's interests and are also close personal friends.

The first member of our family to take office as Master of the Horse was the 4th Earl of Worcester, my ancestor about whom I have already written who was originally responsible for Badminton becoming our home. His was a singularly unexpected and surprising appointment to be made by the bigotedly Protestant Queen, for Worcester was well known to be a staunch Roman Catholic. The fact that Queen Elizabeth chose him to succeed the ambitious Earl of Essex, one of her latter-day-favourites who paid the price of ambition at the axe-man's hand on Tower Hill in 1601, must I think have been because of Worcester's profound love for music and drama. These qualities would have had an immense appeal to the Queen, being as she was a considerable poet and musician in her own right, talents she had undoubtedly inherited from her father, Henry VIII. She explained her choice by saying that Lord Worcester reconciled what up to then she had believed impossible, in that while being a stiff Papist, he remained a loyal subject. These sentiments were put even more graciously by Ludovic Lloyd, Sergeant-at-Arms from 1573 to 1610 when he said: 'She forgave his faith which was Popish, and honoured his faithfulness which was Roman.'

Worcester was a close friend of the poet Spenser, who composed a special ode on the occasion of the double marriage of his two daughters, the Ladies Elizabeth and Catherine Somerset:

> Sure they did not seem
> To be begot of any earthly seed,
> But rather Angels or of Angels' bread;
> Yet were they bred of *Somers-heat* they say.
> Sweet Thames! run softly till I end my song.
> *(Prothalamion)*

He was also a patron of William Byrd, the Roman Catholic Elizabethan composer who seemed also to have overcome the prejudices of the Queen, as he was the main contributor to Queen Elizabeth's 'Virginal Book', a celebrated collection of studies for what was the Queen's favourite musical instrument.

In his role as a prominent patron of drama, my ancestor,

Edward Worcester, brought to Court the company of the renowned comedian, Will Kemp, and he managed to obtain permission for them to act in public theatres at a time when actors were treated little better than thieves and vagabonds unless they were fortunate enough to be able to claim noble patronage – Shakespeare himself being a victim of this ridiculous state of affairs. In fact, it was only when James VI came down from Scotland to be crowned James I of England and put all existing companies under royal protection that this stupidity ended.

By one of those strange quirks of fate that seem to provide a magical link between generations hundreds of years apart, on 21 April 1979, when Queen Elizabeth II celebrated her birthday while she was staying with us at Badminton for the Three-Day Event, I invited a well-known stage and television comedian, Chris Harris, to come and stage an entertainment for her in our Front Hall. When I asked him to come I had no idea that up to then his greatest success had been with a brilliant portrayal of Will Kemp. I wonder if the ghost of the original Will Kemp looked down on us as we rocked with laughter at the antics of the modern Will Kemp performing on an improvised stage in the Front Hall. Perhaps he muttered into his beard: 'Hmm – I used to make my Queen laugh just as much as that!'

Amateur acting, charades and sing-songs have always ranked high among the amusements of our Royal Family, so when the Prince of Wales and Prince Andrew were invited by Chris Harris to help him with the effects, they entered wholeheartedly into the rollicking good humoured spirit of the evening, and the three of them brought the house down with their antics.

My ancestor, the 4th Earl of Worcester, led Queen Elizabeth's favourite palfrey, draped in black velvet, behind the hearse in her funeral procession, and her successor, King James I invited him to remain in office. This he did until 1616 when a new face appeared at court, that of George Villiers, later to be created Duke of Buckingham. A pushing and ambitious man, Villiers superseded Worcester as Master of the Horse, but my ancestor continued in royal service, and was made Lord Privy Seal. Although his appointment to that office may have been in part as a sop to his vanity on being removed from the office of Master of the Horse, the main reason may have been due to his undoubted diplomatic ability. Thirty years before, as a young man, he had been sent to Edinburgh as the Queen's Ambassador to bear her congratulations to her distant cousin, King James VI of Scotland on the occasion of his marriage. It is possible that when the new king was making the appointment, he chose Worcester because he remembered that first time they had met.

Edward Worcester was destined to outlive James I, and he attended Charles I as Lord Chamberlain at his coronation in 1625. But in the March of 1628, that grand old Elizabethan died at Worcester House in London, and was buried at Raglan by the side of his wife. Sadly, she had died four years earlier, and they missed celebrating their golden wedding – a rare occasion in those days – by only four months.

As a family we have had a very long history as Royalists, and Henry Somerset, who succeeded his father as 5th Earl of Worcester and later defended Raglan Castle gallantly, even though unsuccessfully, against Cromwell and his bull-dozing troops, must have been something of a philosopher. In his writings is the following passage which I think contains some very profound thoughts:

> There is nothing so bad as is good for something. If there was no silence, there would be no music, for the sudden stops that are in music add to the grace and perfection of the Art; ignorance is a spur to knowledge; darkness a pavilion to the Almighty; so are afflictions good for our instructions and adversities for our amendments.

With a father who was a patron of the arts, and having himself been educated by the Jesuits, he must have had his literary appetite whetted from early childhood. But of affliction, the poor man certainly had his share, for only six out of his thirteen children grew to maturity.

So the office of Master of the Horse was established as such in the 14th century, and since then there have been seventy-six holders out of all of whom I myself held office for the longest time – just over forty years. A rather grim statistical note is the fact that no fewer than five out of the seventy-six were executed: the Duke of Hamilton, Sir James Tyrrell, Sir Nicholas Carew, the Earl of Essex and the Duke of Monmouth.

In mediaeval times the horse was bound to play a far more important part in the daily lives of everyone, not only of the

Monarch, than it does today. While we have motor cars and aeroplanes to carry us about the world, they relied entirely on the horses as a means of locomotion and as a beast of burden. As the King moved constantly about from one royal residence to another, not only in this country but in France, where he also ruled over vast territories, the duties of his Master of the Horse were bound to be varied and exacting. Those perpetual migrations must have called for very skilled organisation, for not only did all the royal luggage have to be conveyed from place to place (and this not only consisted of clothes, but included everything that the king and his great entourage would need throughout their journeyings, right down to the smallest eating utensils) but provender and shelter had to be arranged *en route* for all the human beings and horses involved in the giant exercise. The saying 'harbingers of doom' has its origins in the necessarily ruthless messengers who were sent on ahead to make sure that everything would be readily forthcoming.

In those far off days, the Master of the Horse was also called upon to provide the King with horses for war, and when one reads that no fewer than ten thousand fighting men with twenty-five thousand horses were assembled at Southampton for shipment to France before Henry V's battle of Agincourt, the duties of the Master of the Horse can have been no sinecure! It was not until nearly three hundred years later, when William of Orange and his wife, Mary, came to the throne in 1689 that the Master of the Horse was relieved of this heavy responsibility.

In the olden days, the duties of the Master of the Horse also included the carrying of the Monarch's standard into battle. When I was in my thirties, that is a job I would positively have enjoyed!

In those days too, it was the Master of the Horse who saw to it that the King was well supplied with all kinds of horses that were needed for a host of pleasures, among them jousting, hunting and racing, and these requirements necessitated the maintenance of large breeding establishments. I must admit that my only personal sortie into the breeding of horses for royal use was when I crossed two Percheron mares with a thoroughbred stallion. The products turned out to be two splendid heavy grey horses, eminently suitable to go to the Royal Mews. We named them Beaufort and Badminton, and Badminton had the distinction of being a member of the team that drew the Coronation Coach in 1953. Poor Beaufort had a sudden heart attack while being led out to grass at Windsor; but he also had had his moment of triumph, for he had been used only the day before to draw the Royal Carriage down the race-course in the colourful procession that precedes each day's racing and gives so much pleasure to the racegoers.

Had I lived in earlier times, one of my duties would have been not only to produce horses for the Sovereign's use in the hunting field – and Henry VIII is said to have got through eight in one day! – but also to arrange and 'attend the Sovereign's pleasures' throughout the day. With great ceremony, the Master of the Horse was required to proffer a stirrup cup as soon as the Monarch was mounted. Although the heir to the throne, Prince Charles, sometimes comes out to have a day's hunting with my hounds, I fear there is scant ceremony when I hand over my flask to him at the end of a good and hard hunt.

In those days I would also have found myself in charge of the Royal buckhounds, otterhounds, hart-hounds and foxhounds. Even though each Royal pack of hounds had its own master or keeper with an independent budget, they nevertheless came under the general supervision of the Master of the Horse.

The duties of the Master of the Horse have varied over the years, but for centuries they included taking responsibility for the Royal Menagerie. At the time of Henry I (1100–1135) many exotic animals that had been sent to him as gifts from foreign potentates were kept at Woodstock in what was to become the first enclosed park in England:

> ... deer, divers strange beasts to be kept and nourished, such as were brought to him from far countries, as lions, leopards, lynxes, porpentines and such other

were all kept in this great tract of land, some thousands of acres in extent, and completely surrounded by high walls. But as gifts continued to pour in for the Norman and Plantagenet kings, those walls were not considered to be safe enough, and the collection was brought to London and housed in what was to be called 'the Lion House' at the Tower of London; a lion-keeper was employed by the man who was still known then as 'the Keeper of the Horse'.

By 1815, when George III was on the throne, the royal menagerie had dwindled to 'one lion, two lionesses, one panther, one hyena, one tigress, one jackal, one mountain cow and one large bear', and seven years later after George IV succeeded, the sole survivor of those nine animals was the poor big bruin, but he had been joined by an elephant and a couple of birds.

Great changes were about to take place, for owing to the enthusiasm and drive of Alfred Cops, the then Keeper, in 1829 a Royal Charter was granted for the opening of a zoo in Regent's Park, coinciding with the founding of the Royal Zoological Society. Five years later, the motley little collection of animals at the Tower of London was removed to its new home, the only livestock remaining being the famous ravens. I am sure that the Duke of Leeds who was Master of the Horse at that time must have heaved a great sigh of relief when the responsibility for the Royal Menagerie was at last removed from his shoulders.

Although I always loved being taken as a treat to the zoo in Regent's Park, my only other connection with a zoo has been with the one at Bristol of which I am a patron. This I have always found a wholly enjoyable task, but I am thankful to say it does not require me to produce six pounds of meat daily for a resident tiger as fell to the lot of one of my luckless eighteenth-century predecessors as Master of the Horse!

Since Hanoverian times, the actual day-to-day running of the Royal Mews has been the responsibility of a member of the Royal Household known as the Crown Equerry; he is now responsible for finding horses for the Queen and other members of the Royal Family and their entourage, not only for State occasions, but when they are riding for leisure and for pleasure.

Nowadays, of course, a fleet of motor cars is also kept in the Royal Mews, and these too are the responsibility of the Crown Equerry. In Queen Victoria's time there were about two hundred horses in the Royal Mews at Windsor and in London, but inevitably with the development and general use of motor cars and aircraft, that number has decreased. Today there are only about thirty carriage horses on active duty. Some of these are older horses that are specially kept for routine day-to-day messenger duties around the streets of London, and they ply to and fro between the Palace, the Treasury and Downing Street, drawing the Royal Brougham on its daily rounds. Every new Ambassador to the Court of St James's is provided with a State Carriage for his or her visit to Buckingham Palace to present the letters of credence to the Queen.

The majority of people in the British Isles do not have much to do with horses, and they may never see them close to except on ceremonial occasions, on the race-course or at a horse-show, so they cannot possibly be expected to have any idea of how much behind-the-scenes work is involved in presenting the polished annual 'performances' such as the Trooping the Colour on the Monarch's official birthday and the State Opening of Parliament. The mere fact that it is possible to train horses to the sort of standard where they will not shy and bolt for five miles, having taken fright at the bunting, the flag-waving and the cheers of the assembled crowds, is in itself a tribute to all the people who have been intimately concerned with their care and training.

There need to be ceaseless and unremitting training and rehearsal sessions, and before a great state ceremony the horses are often being exercised in the streets of London as early as four-thirty in the morning. The staff have to be up even earlier, as it takes a long time to prepare the horses and carriages.

With a head coachman, there are three other coachmen in charge of each of three 'sets' of horses, each of these numbering eight or ten. Their jobs are arduous, for between them these men have to look after not only the horses, but more than eighty carriages and horse-drawn vehicles. The vagaries of the English climate play a large part in determining the amount of work that has to be done, for if two State occasions closely follow one another, then the amount of work is more than doubled if the weather is bad, for every speck of dirt has to be cleaned off everything, the horses, their saddlery, the harness, the coaches and the uniforms, so that all will be ready for use at cock-crow the next morning.

The actual administrative staff is comparatively small, being headed by a Superintendent, responsible to the Crown Equerry for the day-to-day running of the Royal Mews. In mediaeval days there was an official known as an 'avenor' who was responsible for the provisions, but nowadays his job is done by a man known as the Comptroller of Stores. A Chief Clerk with two assistants form a channel of communication between the department and the outside world.

These are the people then who provide us with the splendid pageantry that we all enjoy, and that are so much a part and parcel of our heritage.

My appointment as Master of the Horse was gazetted on 21 July 1936, and I continued in the office for the next forty-one years, when at the end of Queen Elizabeth's Silver Jubilee celebrations, I felt that the time had come for me to step down and make way for a younger man.

When I originally took office, it was at a time of general stress in the Western world, as the might of Hitler with his greedy demands and cruel prejudices was beginning to be felt and understood more clearly all over the continent of Europe. But with the abdication imminent, it was a time of particularly acute strain for the whole of our Royal Family.

When Edward VIII eventually relinquished the throne in favour of his younger brother, the Duke of York, the new King asked me if I would continue in office. Needless to say, I was honoured and delighted to do so.

His Coronation which I attended as Master of the Horse on 12 May 1937, was not the first Coronation in which I had taken part. Way back in 1911, twenty-six years before, when I was still at my private school, I was given leave to attend the Coronation of King George V in order to act as train-bearer to my father, who was to carry the Curtana, or Sword of Mercy, in the great and solemn procession that preceded the actual crowning of the new King at Westminster, and throughout the long service.

Imagine what such an occasion meant in the life of an eleven-year-old boy; for not only was I bursting with pride at the wonderful appearance of my mother and father, but I myself was adorned in finery the like of which I had never before known, even though I had been a page boy at several weddings.

It is not true to say that the male of our species does not enjoy dressing up. The fact is that he does not have nearly enough opportunity to do so. I have always enjoyed the children's Christmas fancy-dress parties we have given at Badminton, and on my eightieth birthday, I held a ball and asked my guests to come disguised as famous racehorses. I went as King Priam of Troy, the racehorse Troy having won the Derby in 1979, and the name Troy of course having such a strong family meaning.

For King George V's Coronation I had an outfit made specially for me by my father's Court Tailors consisting of white satin knee breeches with silk stockings and silver-buckled shiny black shoes. Over a shirt of the finest silk, I wore round my neck a cravat that fell down in ruffles of the most beautiful Brussels lace, with matching cuffs that half-covered my hands. Over all this finery, I wore a beautiful blue satin coat. Small wonder that I felt like a little peacock as I walked solemnly and carefully after my father up the aisle of Westminster Abbey, holding his train high in the air as he moved on slowly before me, bearing that precious sword with its severed top symbolising Mercy, flanked by Lord Roberts, VC, bearing the Sword of Justice to the

Spirituality and Lord Kitchener with the Pointed Sword or Sword of Temporal Justice.

We had risen at day-break that morning, and a hurried breakfast at which I hardly ate or drank anything – I was a little afraid that I might be sick on the way to the Abbey, seated as I would be with my back to horses in our family State Coach which was none too well sprung. This had been specially refurbished and brought up by rail from Badminton for the great day. Alas, it was destined to be a victim of Hitler's blitzkrieg together with all our other coaches and carriages that were on loan to a museum in Bristol that was burnt to the ground on one terrible night when half that old city and docks went up in flames. All that remains is one solitary set of harness hanging in my stud-groom's room in my stables.

The swaying coach was drawn by four horses specially bred for their job. In those days, such animals were far easier to obtain than now, as necessity always creates a supply. Carriage horses must have a minimum height of 16.2 hh, that is to say, they must be 5 ft 6 in high at the withers which is the point at the bottom of a horse's mane. Not only must a team be even in size, but they must also have plenty of bone; in other words, they need to have strong thick legs and, more important still, they must have a straight even action. This is essential if they are to pull together as a team. If one horse lifts its legs too high or has a clumsy action, then it will throw the others out and give the occupants of the coach a very bumpy and uncomfortable ride. Not only do the horses have to draw the coaches, but they also have to carry very heavy accoutrements – it takes two men to lift the head-collars alone on – so that is why they need to be very strongly built.

Judging by the dazzling appearance of the team of horses that awaited us when we emerged from the house on 22 June 1911 to run the gauntlet of the eager gaze of a little crowd of people gathered outside on the pavement, I imagine their grooms must have been up nearly all night, strapping and polishing the horses so that their coats looked like mahogany, and their manes and tails were plaited with ribbons of the family colours woven into them.

How eagerly I had looked forward to the whole affair from the first moment I was told that I was to bear my father's train, and my expectations were more than borne out by the thrilling reality. Not a detail of that Coronation Day has been glamorised by the passage of time, for it was a truly wonderful day from start to finish. Little did I think when I so proudly carried my father's train in Westminster Abbey that at the next Coronation I would attend, I would be Master of the Horse!

The Coronation of King George VI and Queen Elizabeth was one of my first duties in my new office; for although the ceremony of Trooping the Colour had been held the previous summer, the King, Edward VIII, had been unable to attend, so his brother, the Duke of Gloucester deputised for him, and I was not required to be there. The usual Ascot processions instituted by George IV in 1820 had taken place, but this was the first time I was called upon to carry out mounted ceremonial duties in London.

Although the actual details of the procession were more than adequately taken care of by others, the ultimate responsibility was mine, and of course I had taken the greatest care to make sure as far as was humanly possible that nothing could go wrong. Meticulous attention to tiny detail is imperative; even so, something idiotic like one broken strap could well spell disaster on a great occasion. The staff at the Royal Mews have always been chosen for their thoroughness, most of them being recruited from one or other branches of the armed forces where they will have undergone a thorough grounding in both ceremonial procedure and drill.

In the actual Coronation Procession, in my new position as Master of the Horse, I rode a grey charger to the right of the Coronation Coach, immediately behind the Royal Standard, and in front of the Royal Dukes.

When my grandfather as Master of the Horse was riding slowly down the Mall by the side of Queen Victoria's coach in a procession that took place to celebrate her twenty-first year as Queen, he felt a tap on his leg. Quickly turning his head, he saw the tip of the royal umbrella disappearing back inside the open window. It was evident that the Queen had something to say, so he leant down as far as possible to hear. It seemed that the Queen was worried because they were going so slowly – please would my grandfather do something about it? With that speed of decision for which he was renowned, instead of making his way up the side of the procession to reach its head, as nine out of ten others would have done, he urged his horse in a series of spectacular leaps and bounds up the Duke of York's steps that rise in shallow flights connecting the Mall with Carlton House Terrace and the bottom of Lower Regent Street. This bold action brought him to the head of the procession, and having speeded it up, he then calmly waited for the Royal Coach to come along, when he fell in by its side once more, to receive the smiling approbation of his Queen.

All State occasions brought with them their moments of anxiety, but I remember one in 1939, six months before the outbreak of war, that produced more than its fair share of worry. The President of France and his wife, Monsieur and Madame Lebrun, were due to arrive at Victoria by special train, and then to continue their journey in carriage procession to Buckingham Palace.

At five minutes to zero, when the train was expected to steam into the station, the cavalry escort which had had written orders from the Crown Equerry, Sir Arthur Erskine to arrive twenty minutes earlier, still had not come. The troop of Life Guards had had to gear its rate of progress to that of their Colonel's horse, which happened to be a very slow walker, and the young adjutant could hardly urge his superior officer to get a move on.

Meanwhile, on board the train itself, there had been a terrible muddle. It had been arranged that the President and his wife, and high-ranking ministers should change from their travelling clothes into more elegant attire on the train; but they could not find the right suitcases, which were buried under a heap of luggage, for the special labels that had been sent to Paris marked 'Wanted on the Train' had been used by the whole French party.

Eventually the train arrived and greetings were exchanged, but then that ill-fated Guard of Honour fell in immediately after the Royal cars, not giving the Prime Minister and other dignitaries a chance to get away from the station first so that they could be at Buckingham Palace when the President arrived.

However, we were not the only ones to make mistakes, for a reciprocal visit to Paris later that summer was not without its moments of anguish for the French organisers.

They made such elaborate precautions to safeguard the lives of their royal visitors, erecting barriers all along the processional routes that were set so far back from the road that only those fortunate enough to have a seat in a balcony or one of the grandstands that had been put up along the route were able to get even a fleeting glimpse of the King and Queen. Even so, the visit was a dazzling success and the Queen, looking enchanting in the beautiful dresses designed for her by Norman Hartnell, caught the heart of Paris.

One Parisian newspaper reported that a figure in a cocked hat and a scarlet uniform was so impressive that the people at the back of the crowd set up the murmur of *'C'est Lui!'* (That is he!) But I'm afraid it wasn't, for it was me in my uniform as Master of the Horse, and not the King.

I found myself being described in the French newspapers alternately as *'Grand Maitre des Ecuries du Roie'* or by the old French title of *'Grand Ecuyer'*, both of which when roughly translated, just about put me on a par with the King's stud-groom!

Even more amusing was the fact that the Duchess of Northumberland, Mistress of the Robes – an ancient title that is well understood in this country – was described in the French papers as *'Grande Maitresse de la Coeur'* (Great Mistress of the Heart) which is a description open to all manner of misinterpretation, whatever the language! Helen Northumberland, a daughter of the Duke of Richmond and Gordon, was a most distinguished person, quite apart from being extremely good company, and she and I often found ourselves paired off at royal functions.

On the last evening of our stay in Paris, we were all bidden to the Quai d'Orsay for a State Banquet. When we arrived, decked in all our evening finery, we were instructed to watch for a signal, at which we were to take our sides by our dinner partners and process into the enormous banqueting hall in a certain order that would ensure that we went straight to our correct places. When we marched into the hall, we were confronted with a scene of confusion, and found ourselves at the wrong end of an enormous horseshoe-shaped table; there followed an extremely undignified scramble as we ran hither and thither trying to find our correct places.

Another French State Visit which caused me some worry was that of General Charles de Gaulle. I was bidden to escort him on his drive from Buckingham Palace to the Guildhall to pay his respects to the Lord Mayor. I was told that he was a stickler for detail and would want all the places of interest *en route* pointed out. Although I had spent some time in London when I was in the army, that had been a long time before, and a world war had intervened. In any case, the West End of London as viewed by a young subaltern is a very far cry from the City of London as seen by a visiting State dignitary.

However, fortunately I had what proved to be a brilliant idea, for I walked from our Grace and Favour Apartment in Kensington Palace down to Kensington High Street and hailed a taxi. I explained my predicament to the cabby, a real Cockney; true to type, not only was he quick in the uptake, but he was also intelligent and proved to be a mine of information. He drove me slowly along the whole route and pointed out everything of interest, giving me ample time to make copious notes. That evening, I went over my scribblings with a map spread out in front of me checking on the details, and it is a good thing that I did, for, sure enough, General de Gaulle cross-examined me about every building and monument that caught his eye; thanks to that London cabby, as far as I know I was word perfect in my answers.

Not long after the war, Queen Wilhelmina of the Netherlands abdicated in favour of her daughter, Queen Juliana. Following the new Queen's accession, our King and Queen paid a State Visit to Amsterdam; at the banquet held the first evening I talked to Prince Bernhard, and was delighted with the interest he showed in my hounds – so much so that I invited him to come and have a day with me and see for himself how they worked.

To my delight, he took up this invitation, and I am glad to say that it turned out to be one of the best hunting days we have ever had. A comical note was struck by the fact that the Prince did not possess a top hat, so he borrowed one from the Burgomaster of Amsterdam. Unfortunately his head was much bigger than that of Prince Bernhard, so when the Prince was taking a fence, his borrowed hat flew off, and he had to continue the hunt with a bare head. Luckily I found the hat, muddy and squashed, the very next day when I was walking with my dogs, for the Prince had given me a rough idea of where it had been lost. I had it tidied up, and then we posted it back to its rightful owner.

My concern at the outbreak of war was not only with my own estate, but also with what would happen in the Royal Mews. It did not prove possible to move the Royal coaches out of London for two years, and it was not until the autumn of 1941 that the thirteen-foot-high gold Coronation Coach lumbered fifty miles out of London by a route to the north that had been specially chosen in order to avoid low bridges on its way to a specially enlarged coach-house at Mentmore in Buckinghamshire, English seat of the 6th Earl of Rosebery.

That wonderful golden Coronation Coach was commissioned to be built in 1768 by the 3rd Duke of Rutland who was then Master of the Horse. But so elaborate were its decorations (the doors being painted specially by an Italian Florentine artist, Giovanni Cipriani) that it was not finished in time for George

III's Coronation. It cost £7,661 18s 11d, weighed four tons requiring eight horses to draw it along.

It was essential that so valuable an object should be housed somewhere that not only was safe, but also damp-proof. The entire staff of the National Portrait Gallery had been evacuated to Mentmore, together with many of the priceless paintings from that gallery, and they took the coach under their care, mounting a day-and-night guard which was maintained throughout the whole of the war.

The state liveries and harness – difficult enough to replace then, but impossible nowadays – were also sent to a place of safety, and the remaining six State Carriages went to the racecourse at Ascot. They journeyed one at a time, so that in the event of a sudden strafing raid, only one would be in danger of damage or destruction.

At last the war was over, but the horses in the Royal Mews were very depleted. It is necessary for the Crown Equerry to keep a permanent look-out for suitable animals in order to maintain the strength. Not only must he be sure that youngsters are coming on so that the older horses can be replaced, but he has to have a good idea of where the kind of horse he needs is being bred.

Before the war, Yorkshire was the main breeding place of the celebrated Windsor Greys, but when Colonel Dermot Kavanagh, Sir Arthur Erskine's successor, went up there in 1945, it was only to find that the source of supply had completely dried up. Fortunately, and most expediently, Queen Wilhelmina of the Netherlands presented the King with five beautiful grey geldings, describing her generous gift as only a slight recompense for the hospitality we had provided for her when her own country had been overrun by the invading German hordes.

His native Ireland was the next place that Colonel Kavanagh tried, and by the time he and I were discussing the plans for Queen Elizabeth II's Coronation Procession, by one means or another, he had managed to restore the Royal Mews to its pre-war strength.

The Coronation in 1953 was the signal for a good deal of restoration work to be carried out on the Coronation Coach, for in spite of all the loving care that had been lavished upon it during its four-year sojourn at Mentmore, it was inevitable that with the passage of time defects would show. The beautiful Cipriani panels, which had been described by the historian,

28. With H.M. the Queen on Coronation Day. In the Royal Procession it was my duty and privilege to ride immediately behind my Monarch's coach.

29. *Representing King George VI at Lloyd George's Memorial Service, 10 April 1945. During the forty years or so that I was Master of the Horse I frequently represented the Sovereign on official occasions both here and abroad.*

Horace Walpole, two hundred years before as being 'full of improprieties', were restored by skilled artists, and the whole of the rest of its surface was re-gilded by experts at enormous expense. New rubber tyres were specially made, and the velvet cushions, by then threadbare, were replaced. Someone had the bright idea of illuminating the inside of the coach with fluorescent lighting that operated from special batteries; this innovation not only gave a better view of the occupants, but it helped the press photographers as well.

So, for the second time in my life, on 3 June 1953, I took pride of place in the Royal Procession, riding immediately behind my Monarch's coach.

During the forty or so years that I was Master of the Horse, I was sometimes called upon to perform a duty that, strictly speaking, was out of the usual line. One of these occasions led indirectly to my seeing the famous white stallions at the Spanish Riding School in Vienna.

My visit to that wonderful place where a most exquisite performance is staged in what must be the most beautiful ball room in Europe – all white and gold and sparkling with the light from a line of great crystal chandeliers – came about in a totally unexpected and roundabout way. It was 1 April 1947, and I was dressed in the casual sort of clothes that I always wear when busy around the estate – a pair of grey flannel bags with an open-necked shirt and a sports coat. I came into the house to be met by my secretary. He had received an urgent message from Buckingham Palace to say that King George of the Hellenes had died, and the member of the Royal Family deputed to represent the King at the funeral had suddenly been taken ill, so I was required to take his place.

I must admit that for a moment I thought that it might be an elaborate April Fool joke, but I found that a suitcase had already been packed, and a car was waiting at the door to take me to the airport. So, dressed just as I was, off I hurried, my tail coat over my arm; it was not long before I was airborne and bound for Athens.

When we arrived at our destination, the plane circled the airport time and time again, until I began to wonder if there was anything wrong. Then a message was brought to me from the pilot's cabin to say that a military guard of honour would be lined up when I alighted and I would be required to inspect them. It was a moment of panic stations, for what on earth was I to do? There I was, high over Athens dressed for a walk at Badminton with my dogs. Hastily I tore off my sports jacket and grabbed my tail coat – at least that was a start. There remained the problem of my open-necked shirt. Feverishly I looked around the aeroplane; my eye alit on the white silk scarf worn by one of the air crew. Barely stopping to ask his permission, I had it off his neck and round my own in a brace of shakes, and with frenzied fingers, tied it in a semblance of a cravat.

By that time, the plane had landed and come to a halt on the runway. I stepped from it into blinding sunshine, and more or less had to feel my way down the steps, hardly able to see a thing because of the intensity of the light. When I reached the bottom, I was greeted by the English envoy, who must have had a moment's qualm when he saw my bizarre appearance. However, bringing all his diplomatic training to bear on the situation, he accompanied me as I walked slowly between the double lines of Greek soldiers.

It had not occurred to me that they would look totally unlike their British counterparts, but even if it had, I would hardly have been prepared to see them looking like a cross between female ballet dancers and characters from a Gilbert and Sullivan operetta! There were all those tough men lined up and wearing what looked to me like little ballet skirts with red velvet boleros. Why should *I* worry about *my* dress?

Although the occasion was, of course, a solemn one, nevertheless I enjoyed my stay in Athens. I was taken to see all the sights, and while there I had a pair of shoes made in an exact pattern of my own and delivered within twenty-four hours. I wear them to this day.

When I boarded the plane that was to take me home, the pilot met me and said that, as it would be necessary to refuel on the way home, would I like to choose the place? So that is how I came to pay an unexpected visit to the Spanish Riding School in Vienna. My wife, whose father had been a diplomat, had lived in Vienna when she was a child, and had often given me glowing accounts of the Riding School that is tucked away so carefully and so unexpectedly in the heart of Vienna.

When we were over London on our way home, the pilot asked me another question. This time he wanted to know where I would like to land. By that time, my mind was on the next day's hunting, so it was without hesitation that I asked him to go to Lyneham, an airfield that is only a few miles from Badminton.

'How do I get there, Sir?'

'Oh, you just follow the GWR line to Swindon, branch left and you'll see it down below.'

Imagine giving such directions nowadays on a plane that travels at a speed faster than sound!

Another trip abroad, this time to Denmark, gives me amusing memories. The Danes were evidently afraid of their aeroplanes having to make forced landings; before any passengers were allowed on board, they were required to take with them supplies of food for an emergency of that nature. So when I tried to get on my plane, I was sent back posthaste to the airport restaurant to collect a packet of sandwiches!

The decision to give up my office as Master of the Horse, caused me the deepest of heart searching. Although naturally I miss it all, I am absolutely certain that I did the right thing. My successor, David, Earl of Westmorland, is so near to me in build and in height, that I was able to hand over all my uniform to him, even my boots, and it all fits him without a single alteration having been necessary.

It is typical of the understanding and warm-heartedness of the Queen that just before the Ascot week immediately following my resignation I received a message asking me to contact the Palace. When I did so, it was to learn that the Queen had personally asked if I would care to go up to Windsor and deputise for David Westmorland, who had to go abroad on business.

So it was with a real sense of pride that I found myself seated once again in the carriage, facing my Sovereign, as it went down that lovely course in exactly the same way as I had done for so many years before.

When I sit at my desk in my room at Badminton, I look up to see a picture of me in my uniform as Master of the Horse, mounted on a fine grey horse that I rode for several years. This was a portrait painted especially by Terence Cuneo and given to me by the Queen as a memento of the years during which I had the honour of serving three Monarchs. When the Queen first suggested it, I readily agreed to sit for the portrait, but asked if she and Prince Philip could also be in the picture.

As I look at that picture, the memories – all of them happy ones – come flooding back.

From a daily newspaper at the time of the Coronation:

A friend of mine and his wife were among the huge

crowd that watched the Coronation in the Mall. They found themselves next to a most cheery Londoner and they were soon on Christian name terms with him.

My friends had a programme so they were able to answer his questions as to who was who. When the Duke of Beaufort passed, they told him that he was the Master of the Horse. He said, 'But I thought Gordon Richards had got the job.'

CHAPTER EIGHT

QUEEN MARY AT BADMINTON

When the first murmurs of pending trouble were heard, and Hitler continued the 'take-overs' that had started with his annexation of Czechoslovakia in March 1939, we heard from Buckingham Palace that should there be a war, then Queen Mary would come down to Badminton to stay with us. As the situation in Europe worsened, I made all the arrangements that I could so that I could be free to re-join my old Regiment, the Blues, at a moment's notice. As I expected to be away from Badminton for some considerable time – no one knew how long – I naturally had an elaborate programme to get through, and it all had to be done in double quick time. One cannot hand over an estate like Badminton with an entirely sanguine heart, and not only did I have to make emergency arrangements for the estate, but I also had to ensure that suitable and adequate arrangements were also made for my kennels and stables.

I did all that I possibly could in the limited time at my disposal, and I duly presented myself at the barracks. During 1939, while Germany had spent £1,710 million, a quarter of her whole national income, on armaments, in this country we had spent a mere £358 million, which represented only 7 per cent of our own national income; even so, this was a far greater sum than that spent by our ally, France. Plans were hastily made by Sir John Anderson, who later became Lord Waverley, for the evacuation of women and children from the cities, for the provision of air-raid shelters, for the distribution of gasmasks to all civilians, for emergency fire and transport services, and for the involvement of many voluntary organisations.

But, while all this had been done, no plans whatsoever had been made for the reception of large numbers of ex-officers who flooded into the barracks of the Household Cavalry! Not only was there no food and no accommodation, but quite simply, there was nothing for us to do.

So, having fully expected to be sent almost immediately across the Channel to fling myself into the fight against Hitler, it was with an undoubted feeling of anti-climax that I found myself instead three days later at the covert-side at seven o'clock in the morning just as I always had been in September. There was I, hunting my hounds as usual, having steeled myself to accept danger and the possibility of sudden death, for I felt certain, in common with the majority of people in the British Isles, that this war would follow the same pattern as that of the Great War of 1914–18 when most young men of the age-group just above mine had been blown to pieces in the trenches – my own half-brother having lost his life on the Somme in the holocaust of 1915.

A month or so later, we received what to us at Badminton was the horrifying news that the R.A.F. were proposing to build a runway right across in front of the house. In the circumstances, we realised that there was absolutely nothing to be done but to grin and bear it, accepting it as one of the sacrifices it is necessary to make when one's country has its back against the wall. But I must admit that we did feel in our heart of hearts that such a desecration of our historic house must surely be unnecessary and that it would be possible to find a much more suitable site for such an air-strip near by, and not absolutely on our doorstep, for Badminton lies on a high plateau that abounds in flat open spaces.

However, that very afternoon we received the doubly welcome news that Queen Mary was going to arrive very shortly to stay with us for an indefinite visit. Not only were we delighted to receive our royal visitor for her own sake, but her arrival put paid to the plans to make an R.A.F. runway in our front garden!

It was therefore with a great sense of relief that I eventually left Badminton to join my unit, for not only was I going to have a chance to do my bit for my country, but I was leaving secure in the knowledge that Queen Mary was settling in happily.

At the end of 1970 I had a letter from a Mr Davies who said he lived right down in the southernmost tip of Wales, and although I probably would not remember, he had in fact met me during the war. He also said that at one time he had been in charge of the Calpe Hunt. Whereas I am afraid that I did not in fact remember meeting him, his mention of the Calpe Hunt interested me very much.

In 1861, my grandfather was told by his doctors that he ought to winter abroad, so he and my grandmother decided to go to Gibraltar. On the face of it, Gibraltar sounds an unlikely place for anyone to wish to spend a winter, and more especially my grandfather, dedicated as he was like the rest of the family to hunting. They went to the Hotel Europa where accommodation had been arranged for them by a cousin of his, Colonel Poulett Somerset of the Coldstream Guards who was later to become M.P. for Monmouth. It is then that one realises that there was an excellent reason for my grandfather's seemingly rather strange choice, for Colonel Somerset had founded a pack of hounds called the Calpe, and the earliest hound list in existence dated November 1859, is headed by the name of a dog-hound, Beaufort, that had been drafted from Badminton the previous season.

When my grandparents journeyed out to Gibraltar they took with them not only twenty couple of hounds for the Calpe Hunt, but also my grandfather's First Whipper-in, Dick Christian, who, mixing these Badminton hounds with the Calpe hounds that were already kennelled on the Rock, showed some excellent sport for those who were able to keep up with him. It is reported that after the splendid hunt from First Ravine (they hunted, of course, on the mainland of Spain) Christian's horse dropped dead under him. I am surprised to find that my grandfather was neither listed as a member of the Hunt, nor is there any reference made to him in any of the records that still exist. However, he undoubtedly continued to take a great interest in the garrison pack, for some years later, over a period of five consecutive seasons, he presented twenty-four-and-a-half more couple of hounds to them – these no doubt being in part gifts to his fourth son, Lord Edward Somerset who was stationed at Gibraltar in 1875 when he was twenty-two under the command of his second-cousin, Major General E. A. Somerset, who was also Chairman of what by then had become the 'Royal' Calpe Hunt.

In my sitting-room at Badminton there hangs a life-sized painting of my grandparents by Sir Francis Grant. It is a truly magnificent picture that dominates the room, and it shows my grandfather mounted on a dapple grey with two of his favourite hounds, and my grandmother on a pretty little bay Andelusian mare called Mazagan. When my grandfather spent that winter in Gibraltar he had earmarked this horse for his wife, and when it was eventually brought home to England by Mr Wynne

Griffith of the 7th Fusiliers, who had himself kept all the Calpe hound records, it had won no fewer than sixteen races.

With my grandparents' picture on the wall beside me, I went on reading Mr Davies's letter with interest, and it brought back many memories, though it was in itself very sad, for he ended by saying that having been badly wounded on the Somme before he was eighteen, he had recently had to have fourteen operations and was now bedridden, being unable to walk a yard without crutches. All his contemporary friends and relations were dead, and now he lived alone, having to rely on someone to go down to the village once a week to fetch his old-age pension. I must say I wonder what happened to the poor chap in the end, though he ended his letter by saying that he had had lots of fun in his life, so what the hell!

By one of those strange quirks of fate, I found that the surgeon who performed all those operations on him was the same one who once saved my own life by doing an emergency tracheotomy on my throat which stopped me from choking with blood after a heavy fall on my head.

I recently heard an amusing little sequel to this incident, for evidently still dangerously ill, I was rushed into a hospital in Bristol. One of the staff was sent for to listen to my breathing; as she came into my room, she noticed a very tall lean figure waiting outside. My condition was fair, but I was by no means out of danger. As she left the room again, the tall stranger who was still leaning on the wall outside, stopped her and asked her if he could possibly go in for a moment to speak to me, as he had something very urgent to say. Knowing how serious was my condition, she naturally thought that he had a last message for me, so she thought she had better allow him to go in for a moment or two, but she went in too to see that he did not stay too long.

You can imagine her amazement, when, instead of exchanging soulful last words, I slowly opened my eyes, and on seeing my visitor, asked eagerly, if faintly: 'Well, Gerald, what did hounds do after I left?' It was then that she realised my visitor was Gerald Gundry, my Joint Master.

But back to Mr Davies's long letter. He told me that he had been in the Army Catering Corps during the last war; one day when he was stationed in London, after delivering a lecture to various London-based Messing Officers at the RASC, Perivale, he was glad to be offered a lift back into town by one of them. On the way up Western Avenue, they stopped for a half-a-crown luncheon in one of the 'gin-palace' type pubs that used to abound along that road, and the conversation took the usual form of question and answer. Mr Davies asked the Captain if he lived in London. 'Not really,' was his reply. 'My home is out in the country in Gloucestershire.'

'So you miss the bombing then?'

'No, not entirely. Last week the Luftwaffe dropped one on my lawn.'

'How did they come to pick on you?'

The unexpected and totally conversation-stopping reply to that innocent question was: 'I expect Hitler found that my wife's aunt was staying with us.'

Mr Davies could well be excused for thinking that his benefactor must have a screw loose, for why on earth should Hitler choose his wife's aunt as his 'target for tonight'?

What Mr Davies did not know at the time, of course, was that I was the Captain who had given him a lift, and my wife's aunt did in fact live with us at Badminton; but as my wife's aunt happened to be Queen Mary, then there was every reason for her to be picked upon by the Luftwaffe!

As I re-read that letter which I had stuck into the pages of my notebooks, I was reminded vividly of the outbreak of the last war.

Queen Mary had duly arrived at Badminton, bringing with her a retinue that consisted of several of her own personal servants, a lady-in-waiting – these ladies did turn-about duties, changing every two or three weeks or so – her Private Secretary, the Hon. Sir John Coke (a brother of the Earl of Leicester), and an Aide-de-Camp, who also changed from time to time. Queen Mary's servants were, I must say, a very welcome addition to our own very depleted domestic labour force, though naturally they had special duties in regard to the Queen. We turned over a set of rooms to Queen Mary on the Church side of the house, in the south-east corner, the set of rooms now occupied by the Queen when she comes to stay at Badminton each year for the Three-Day Event. Although Queen Mary had these private quarters to which she could withdraw if she wished, she did in fact spend most of her leisure time with my wife while I was away on military service.

Eager to make the place as safe as possible for our distinguished guest, we made all sorts of suggestions. Should a special set of air-raid shelters be built well away from the house? Should the whole place be cordoned off for security? But no – the only concessions for her personal safety that Queen Mary would allow was the reinforcement of the ceiling of one of the ground-floor rooms (the one where my mother had habitually inter-viewed the staff each morning thirty years earlier). She agreed, albeit reluctantly, that a squadron of the Gloucestershire Hus-sars should be quartered in the Old Laundry that lies nearly opposite the step door.

For her dining-room, Queen Mary used one of our ground-floor sitting-rooms, a square room on the south side of the house. This room is lined with beautiful Jacobean black oak diamond panelling which originated at Raglan Castle, was taken from there to Troy when Cromwell destroyed Raglan, and even-tually brought to Badminton by my grandfather. This is a room that tends to give visitors rather a surprise, standing as it does right in the centre of what is in the main an eighteenth-century Palladian house.

Queen Mary was seventy-two when she came to live with us, and she had not lived in the country since she was a girl. Even then, I suspect it was not really 'country' in our sense of the word. Therefore, it was only natural that she found the way of life a little strange at first; but it took a lot to daunt Queen Mary, and she set about her new life with a will to learn, soon grasping the difference between oats and barley and all manner of other things that country dwellers take for granted. In fact, so apt a pupil was she, that by the time she left Badminton, she was quite capable of discussing fat-stock prices with the local farmers in a totally authoritative way, taking a genuine interest in the whole subject.

All the same, she felt very restless at the outset of her stay. For one thing, nobody knew how long the war was going to last, and for another, she was totally unaccustomed to a life of inactivity; she had, after all, been a prominent and extremely hard-working member of the Royal Family for nearly fifty years, having married King George V, when heir-apparent to the throne in 1893, at the age of twenty-five. She was even heard to say that she felt as displaced as any Birmingham evacuee.

Fortunately it was not long before her son, King George VI, got wind of his mother's discomfiture, and was swift to act. In the most tactful way possible, he saw to it that from then on the Foreign Office news summaries were sent down to her in Gloucestershire by special messenger each day. They arrived at Badminton in an official red-leather despatch box, the key to which she kept on her person at all times. One day in July 1943, when that important box arrived back in London it was found to contain a note in the Queen's own handwriting: 'From Mary R. The lock of this box is very stiff!'

Queen Mary never had been, and certainly never would be by that time in her life, the sort of character who would be content to sit and read or sew, or perhaps just sit and meditate. She was essentially a woman of action, and it was a downright necessity for her constantly to be on the move doing things. So it was not long before she became a familiar figure in the locality, paying unexpected and most welcome visits to hospitals in Tidworth, Bath and Bristol, where she talked to wounded soldiers, thus helping to relieve the monotony of their days. She was a most popular visitor with all the evacuee children for miles round, as she always had a very special empathy with young people, and her many surprise visits also lightened many a dreary day in local factories and canteens.

Whenever her youngest surviving son, George, Duke of Kent, who was in the Training Command, R.A.F. had occasion to come to the West Country in the course of his duties, he always made a point of visiting his mother; off they would go to Bath to visit the many antique shops that have always abounded in that ancient city. Queen Mary had a profound love for and knowledge of antiques, and her memory was truly remarkable. Once she had seen something that interested her, she never seemed to forget it; years later she would manage to re-unite pairs of tables or sets of chairs in an almost uncanny way. She had such an unerring eye combined with an acquisitive nature, that, so I am told, if local antique dealers got wind of a forthcoming visit from Queen Mary, they hid away their best pieces – that is, any they did not wish to part with, for it would undoubtedly be those which would interest the Queen.

On her arrival, after a few days of comparative idleness, she turned her attention to things that immediately caught her eye in her new environment; as she regarded ivy as an enemy, destructive both to trees and to masonry, she set herself the task of clearing it from the trees in the park and also from the outside of our house. She formed what she called her own 'Ivy Squad'; an entry in her diary on 25 September 1939 reads:

> Lovely morning, which we spent clearing ivy off the trees in the grounds, while Jack Coke [this, of course, was the Hon. Sir John Coke, her Private Secretary, then a man of about sixty years of age, who had led a

fairly sedentary life during the previous few years] hacked the branches off two chestnut trees and an elm not far from the house, and the gardeners began to clear a wall of ivy near Mary B's bedroom. [Mary B of course was my wife.]

A year later, Queen Mary's Ivy Squad, its task completed, became the 'Wooding Squad', and into this new squad she recruited not only her four official despatch riders, but also all the men belonging to the squadron from the Gloucestershire Hussars whose special duty it was to guard her while she stayed with us at Badminton. Nor were her personal staff left out. They were given the command to don old clothes and be ready outside the house early next morning, so when the soldiers marched smartly down Worcester Avenue, they were followed by Queen Mary sitting in a farm cart that I had specially fitted out with basket chairs and which was drawn by two horses.

My wife, on first seeing it, remarked that it looked altogether too much like a tumbril from the French Revolution for her liking, to which remark her Royal Aunt replied sharply:

'Well, it may come to that yet. One never knows!'

It was precisely because one never did know that Queen Mary was being kept as safe as possible at Badminton.

Queen Mary's Wooding Squad tackled an area of sixteen acres in extent, lying on the north side of the house, just outside the limits of the Park. It was named then and is still known as Queen Mary's Plantation.

It was a hot and dishevelled band of courtiers who returned to the house each night at the end of a long day's work; for first they had been required by their Royal task-mistress to wield axe and saw, and then the spades and pick-axes had to come into action. There tended to be an ugly rush into the house, for they had to queue for a bath, as not only was hot water in short supply, but also nobody was supposed to have a bath that was more than five inches deep during the war. Doubtless they recalled wistfully those halcyon days of yesteryear when a dressing bell would ring, and they would then stop whichever activity had been occupying their time, and saunter upstairs to have a bath of whatever depth they chose, in which they could soak for as long as they pleased, before donning evening clothes and returning downstairs to have a cocktail before dinner.

As Queen Mary would never think of sparing herself, it never occurred to her to spare her staff, whatever might be their ages or their infirmities – and the combined ages of her wartime courtiers must have been considerable.

That there was a royal precedent for this sort of attitude is evidenced if one goes back a couple of hundred years to the reign of King George III. This monarch had Tuesdays and Saturdays as his regular hunting days, and like Queen Mary's husband, George V, he was a stickler for punctuality. 'Critically exact to time' he would arrive, attended by his Master of the Horse, equerries and guests. He was well attended for he was known to be a really reckless rider, who threw caution to the winds; as he was full of bravado and not a particularly good horseman, his staff were terrified of what might be the consequences of one of the leaps he urged his mount to make, regardless of the size of the obstacle.

One of his equerries, Colonel Goldsworthy, described in humorous detail exactly what it was like to do his job, expected as he was to accompany his royal master and ride in his pocket, so to speak:

> Being wet over head, soused through under feet, and popped into ditches, and jerked over gates, what lives we do lead! Well, it's all honour, that's my only comfort . . . Home we come, like so many drowned rats . . . sore to the very bone, and forced to smile at the time! And then after that what do you think follows? 'Here, Goldsworthy,' cries his Majesty: so up I come to him, bowing profoundly, and my hair dripping down to my shoes: 'Goldsworthy,' cries his Majesty. 'Sir,' says I, smiling agreeably, with the rheumatism just creeping up all over me, but still expecting something a little more comfortable. I wait patiently to know his gracious pleasure, and then, 'Here, Goldsworthy, I say,' he cries, 'will you have a little barley water?' Barley water after a whole day's hard hunting! [*Diary and Letters*, Mme d'Arblay, iii, 67]

Without a doubt Goldsworthy was not only uttering the feelings of all the long-suffering fellows who attended George III, but also those of many of their successors who have devoted their lives to the service of their Royal masters. But it is evident that his self-pitying complaint by no means conceals his underlying devotion to the King.

While Queen Mary was conducting her land work, I was still

in the Army, though I was invalided out in 1943 after having spent a long time in hospital undergoing an operation for acute gastric ulcers, which put me out of action for a long time. From fifteen stone, I went down to nine and, standing 6ft 4in high, you can imagine what a scarecrow I must have looked; all the same I was not prepared for the reaction of one of my friends. On my way home, I met her when she was shopping in a local town. Taking one look at me she burst out laughing. Extremely puzzled, I asked her the reason for her mirth. 'You look so terribly funny,' was her reply. I must say I was rather hurt, but soon forgave her, and she and her husband remain two of my best friends to this day.

When I got back to Badminton after such a long stay in hospital I set to work to devote myself to organising the Home Guard in the country, and to my estate duties. I took up these tasks reluctantly, as I had been so looking forward to a far more active part in the war, as there was nothing I wanted more than to have the chance to fight for my King and my beloved country. However, we tried to run the estate as economically and efficiently as possible, so that we could produce as much food for the nation as could be squeezed out of every acre that had been put under the plough; it was then that we reduced the size of the Park. That land has never been taken back again, but still produces annual crops of wheat, oats and barley.

During those long war years my wife took upon herself the care of a dozen Guernsey cows, no mean task for a woman single-handed; this meant that she had to rise each morning at an unearthly hour, and then was not free until after the evening's milking had been completed. She has always loved animals, our house at all times being stuffed full of dogs of every variety, but mostly mongrels and several of them from the Battersea Dogs' Home of which I myself have been President for many years. We have had several well-bred Pekinese, and my present terrier's pedigree goes back to those bred by Parson Jack Russell in the middle of the last century. My wife is particularly fond of birds; but this disposition, having become well-known locally, has led to an over-population of her aviary; for when she has opened bazaars and similar fund-raising functions the organisers have rather too often come up with the bright idea of presenting her with a bird rather than with a bouquet.

A journalist from a midlands newspaper once lunched with us at Badminton, and in her written account said that as we lunched, there came a loud whistle through the door. Startled, she asked what it was. 'Psalm 23, I think,' was my wife's quick and unexpected reply, adding that we had a very religious parrot. But that psalm-singing parrot was not as eccentric as one of our previous ones, who led us into all sorts of difficult situations, being, as he was, a veritable Houdini amongst birds. Nearly every day we would get telephone calls from miles around saying that he had been found perched in their hen coop busily pecking away at the chickenfeed, keeping the rightful feeders away. He always returned each night, flying up the Avenue with an attendant retinue of rooks and crows; then the moment he had safely landed in home territory, he would turn round and slate them all, summoning up his considerable vocabulary of invective to do so. It was his knowledge of the worst sort of swear words that led us to take great care to see that he was locked in his cage on Sundays, for on one never-to-be-forgotten occasion, halfway through the sermon, he had flown into the church and settling high up far from anyone's reach, had then proceeded to disrupt the service and disturb the Vicar by his profane remarks, though I must admit that both clergyman and congregation dissolved into fits of mirth.

During the war, in the same way as in every other home in the land, our evenings at Badminton were dominated by the nine-o'clock news, and every night at about five minutes to nine, Queen Mary used to withdraw to her sitting-room, so that she could switch on the wireless and hear the good or bad news in privacy. A royal life does not lend itself very much to a private life, and an entry I once made in my notebooks is very apposite:

We bless our fortune when we see,
our own beloved privacy.

The life of a duke does not lend itself to privacy very much either, and that is perhaps why I value the time I spend fishing in comparative solitude on the banks of the Wye, where I enjoy not only the sport, but I also revel in the feeling of freedom – no telephone, no urgent messages, just the ever-constant and hopeful feeling that sooner or later one may feel that wonderfully welcome tell-tale pull on the line signalling that a fish has taken the fly. Both the Queen Mother and Prince Charles, whom she taught, are excellent fishermen, and perhaps basically their love of the sport which is essentially a solitary one derives from much the same source as my own.

Queen Mary was extremely interested in and knowledgeable about trees and plants, but an endeavour she made to bring her forestry nearer to home, our home, was doomed to failure. She constantly complained that insects were flying into her private rooms, the inference being that they came from the old cedar tree that grows in all its magnificence outside the Oak Room and is part and parcel, not only of that piece of our garden, but also in a way of the family history. It is reported that when that mighty tree can only have been a sapling, it was jumped over by the youngest son of the then Duke of Beaufort, Lord FitzRoy Somerset who, born in 1788, was destined to become Lord Raglan of the perhaps slightly dubious fame of the Charge of the Light Brigade. The windows of my wife's suite of rooms look out on to the upper branches of that tree, and she delights in the bird life that it contains and that can be seen so well from there.

However, Queen Mary had taken against it. She thought that it was too big and altogether too overpowering and therefore it should be removed forthwith. She was determined to have that old cedar tree down. But she had not reckoned on the opposition she would find. My wife was equally determined that the tree should remain, and it must be remembered that the two women came from the same family; in many ways the characters of aunt and niece were remarkably similar!

One day, when Queen Mary had been niggling away at what had almost become her favourite subject, all of a sudden my wife lost her temper. Standing up, she declared that if that tree went, then it would be over her dead body. Staring her Royal Aunt in the eye for a moment, she turned on her heel and rushed out of the room. From that day, nothing more was ever said, and the tree remained unscathed, where I am happy to say it has flourished and still stands forty years later, a monument to my wife's determination.

Queen Mary naturally invited many friends and relations to visit her, for although she was living with a part of her family and there were plenty of people around, she was in fact separated from her nearest and dearest. The King and Queen had elected to stay in London for the duration, visiting Windsor at the weekends where their two daughters, Princess Elizabeth and Princess Margaret Rose were continuing their education, and Queen Mary's younger sons were on active service. Nevertheless, Queen Mary was the sort of woman who could be guaranteed always to fill her life with interests. Even if she had found herself cast up on a desert island, she would probably

30. *With me are* (l. to r.) *Mary, Mrs Roosevelt, Queen Mary, The Princess Royal, 4 November 1942.*

31. *One of Queen Mary's 'Wooding Squads' during the Second World War.*

32. *The Queen sometimes likes to ride when she visits Badminton. This occasion was in April 1959.*

have looked round to get her bearings, and then would have briskly marshalled the natives into a version of her Badminton Wooding Squad, so that, instead of their collecting wood for a fire on which to roast her, they would have found themselves busy looking for a suitable tree to chisel out to make a boat in which to row her to the mainland, singing English sea-shanties instead of native war songs. What is more, I am absolutely certain that they would have been delighted to do so, and tales of the great white Queen would have gone down in their folklore.

We had many visits from interesting and well-known foreigners who were temporarily banished from their own countries and had been offered refuge in these islands. One of the most colourful of these was the diminutive King of Abyssinia, Emperor Haile Selassie (in those days known as the Lion of Judah), who spent the war years in a house just outside Bath, about twelve miles away.

There was one extremely amusing incident which still makes me smile when I think of it. We had invited a Bishop to luncheon, thinking that he would help to entertain Queen Mary, but what we had not known was that the poor man was stone deaf, and therefore found himself at a great disadvantage seated as he was on the right hand of Queen Mary. As has always been the practice in our house, the dogs were in their usual places, two or three under the table, one sitting on a chair next to my wife, and another little terrier hopefully begging by the Bishop's side, a beseeching look in his eyes.

We always had a small dish of dog biscuits placed on the dining-table specially for the dogs, so that we had something suitable to give them when their attentions became a little too pressing. So Queen Mary, by now well indoctrinated in the ways of our household, reached a hand out automatically for one of these biscuits. As the dog had taken up his place out of her reach, on the other side of the Bishop, she handed the little offering to him with a request that he would very kindly drop it into the dog's ever-ready mouth. But, being so deaf, the poor man couldn't hear a word that she said, and evidently thinking that she was recommending him a special titbit, he popped the dog biscuit into his own mouth, and then manfully chewed it. When he had gulped down the last crumb, he turned to Queen Mary and murmured how delicious it had been.

Queen Mary had not had the benefit of a Royal training for nothing, and she did not twitch a muscle, which is more than can be said for the other people seated around the luncheon-table, for they found it quite impossible to conceal their mirth. Fortunately the Bishop could not hear them, but they received withering looks from the Queen; I am glad to say that I myself was able to bend down to feed my own dog that sat at my feet, and was thus able to hide my face.

Dogs have always played an important part in our lives and for many years now I have been privileged to be President of the Dogs' Home at Battersea, which is perhaps better known to the general public as the Battersea Dogs' Home, a position my father also held for a few years. The fate of stray dogs left to roam the hard, hard streets of London is a cause that is naturally very near to the hearts of both my wife and myself. Many years ago now, though it still seems just like yesterday, we received a telephone call from the man who was then in charge of the Home. He said he had a request to make on behalf of a dog, thus getting our immediate attention!

It seemed that a man convicted of some felony had been sent to Dartmoor Prison leaving behind a dog that was therefore likely to have a very long stay at the Home. Could I make any suggestions? Of course, I knew at once what was expected of me, and rose straight to the bait. To cut the story short, Bobo arrived a day or two later, and it was not long before she had become not only the apple of my eye, but also had won the hearts of everyone in my household. She was only a black and white sheep-dog but she had an enchanting character. It is often said that in a man's life there is only one dog and one horse that has pride of place, and Bobo was certainly the dog that took the prize as far as I was concerned. Even today, many years after her death, I cannot think of her without feeling emotion.

When the time came for her master to be released from gaol, we did not know what to do, for surely such a man would not be able to offer her the sort of home to which she had become accustomed, with the certainty of regular food, exercise, warmth and comfort? My wife, a little impetuously, decided to take matters into her own hands, and so she drove with my chauffeur down to Dartmoor, where she met the man as he was released from the prison. Over a cup of tea in a local café they discussed the fate of his pet. To my wife's great relief, and of course to mine when I heard the story later, the man readily agreed that the dog was better off where it was, and it was evident that all he wanted was the best thing for his dog.

My wife told him that we would put a sum of money to his credit in a certain bank account, so that he would have something to fall back on, but to the best of my knowledge that money was never touched.

Since Bobo's time, we have had two other dogs from the home. One was a dear little miniature Pekinese, which caught our eye when we attended the Centenery Celebrations at the Dogs' Home. Named Pity Me by my wife, she was well nigh perfect, her only fault being, that if we took our eyes off her for an instant, she was out of the front door and off across the Park before you could say 'Collar and Lead'. It is all very well if a dog does that in, say, a London garden. No damage is done, and it is soon brought back, but when you think of the vast extent of land that lies outside our front door, little wonder that we were constantly on the alert to see that she had no opportunity to escape. Poor Pity Me spent a good deal of her time sitting in a big cat basket with a proper door made of wire netting out of which she was unable to escape. Sad was the day when she came to an end.

We also have a dog from the Home who rejoices in the name of Tory, as he came to live with us on the day after the Tories came into power under the leadership of Edward Heath. We did think of calling him 'Ted', but as my cousin and heir, David Somerset, has a son called Edward, generally known as Eddie, we thought this might possibly lead to some confusion. That dog was a tiny, tiny puppy when we took it, and we had no way of knowing whether it would grow to reasonable proportions, or become the size of a St Bernard. Tory became redder and redder and more and more like a fox as the months went by, but I am glad to say so far he has not been mistaken for one by my hounds!

All my dogs enjoy hunting rabbits, and every day I take them out and indulge them in this pastime.

My other favourite is little Ajax, a Jack Russell type terrier, who is, in fact, a direct descendant of that sporting parson's breed. Jack Russell, contrary to popular belief, never bred for looks, but only for working ability. If he saw a likely looking terrier, he would buy it; then if it came up to his expectations when it was entered to fox, he would breed from it. Many of the dogs that people loosely call 'Jack Russells' nowadays could never in a hundred years be entered to fox and come out of the earth alive. I have my dog's pedigree dating back to the 1860s, as his forebear was given to my grandfather by a Miss Guest who had an extensive kennel of such dogs descended originally from Jack Russell's terriers in Devon.

Alas, in spite of her catholic tastes, Queen Mary showed little or no interest in either hunting or in my hounds, though she became quite excited one morning when hounds actually killed their fox at the foot of her abhorred cedar tree right outside the house. In this respect she was not like other members of her family, both before and since.

I well remember that when I was about nine, and must just have come home for the Easter holidays, we received a message from London one afternoon to say that the Queen, then of course Queen Alexandra, wife of King Edward VII and therefore Queen Mary's mother-in-law, wished to come down to Badminton to see a Meet of my father's hounds. She had her younger sister staying with her, Dagmar, Empress Maria Fëdorovna of Russia, mother of the last Tsar who was later to be so savagely executed with all his family.

The prospect of having two reigning Queens at a Meet of our hounds was a thrilling one, but it meant that my father had to make swift plans. The Meet the following day had been advertised as being at Joyce's Pool, Didmarton, but naturally my father wanted to have the best possible place for his Royal guests, and what could be better than Worcester Lodge? With its great vista down the Avenue, it would provide a really spectacular and splendid setting for such a rare and historic sporting occasion.

Our two Royal guests arrived quite early in the morning by special train, and they were met at Badminton Station by my father and brought back to the House for rest and refreshment. They had had to leave Buckingham Palace at seven o'clock that morning in order to arrive at Badminton in time to be taken to the Meet in an open Victoria up the Avenue, which my father had hurriedly arranged to have prepared and rolled the evening before. As it was long before the day of universal telephones, my mother's elder brother, my Uncle Bill Harford, was sent off post-haste to Didmarton to warn the Field what had happened, and to bid them to come on to Worcester Lodge. Unfortunately this plan backfired a little, for my uncle was a notorious practical joker and, as luck would have it, this great day was the first of April. It is natural therefore that when Uncle Bill came cantering up to the waiting horsemen and women, and bade them to make haste and go to Worcester Lodge, they just laughed and told him to go off and try his April Fool tricks on somebody else. Fortunately his second horseman had ridden with him, and it was he who eventually managed to persuade them all that this time my uncle was not joking.

Another reason why my father had chosen Worcester Lodge on that particular day was because his Head Keeper, Fred Young, had told him only the morning before that not only had he seen a fox there, but he also knew its habits and where it was certain to be found.

It was therefore with great confidence that my father strode up to Queen Alexandra who, herself a most competent photographer, had been busy helping her sister, the Empress, to take pictures of the Meet, and beckoned her to accompany him. Although obviously a little mystified, she obediently followed him to the foot of a magnificent tree; then, following his instructions, she reached out with her umbrella and tapped its base. To her utter amazement, and to the great delight of the assembled crowd – all the riders by now having arrived from Didmarton which is not far down the road – out jumped a fox who made off at great speed. Hurriedly my father mounted his horse and gave a signal for the huntsman to lay his hounds on to the line. Off they all sped with a lovely cry, followed full pelt by the Field, heading towards Sopworth Brake.

The two Queens hastily got into the Victoria, and their coachman then drove them round the roads to try to give them a glimpse of hounds running. Fortunately he was able to do much more than that, for much to their delight, the fox, a good one, ran past Sopworth Brake, then turning back to Luckley Brake, and was caught in the road by Ragged Castle right in front of their carriage. My father presented the brush to the Empress of Russia, who later wrote to tell him that she had had it mounted as a bellpull.

Some years later, when I was in the army and hunting my own bitch pack whenever I could get away, the Prince of Wales, later Edward VIII, took a house called Easton Grey for a couple of seasons so that he could hunt with our hounds. Standing just off the Sherston–Malmesbury road, Easton Grey is a beautiful eighteenth-century house in a very attractive setting with a fine outlook. Its present owners, Mr and Mrs Peter Saunders and their four children all hunt with me. In 1922 the Prince of Wales rode one of his own horses to victory in a race at our Point-to-Point, and his younger brother, the Duke of Gloucester, also came down to Easton Grey several times and enjoyed many a day's hunting with us.

Queen Mary's own husband, King George V, while still Prince of Wales, had attended a Meet at Worcester Lodge in 1904, and my father mounted him on a horse of my mother's called the Goat. The records show that they had a good day and hounds ran well, but I am afraid that I myself have no recollection of the day at all, as of course I was only four years old.

Our present Queen once had a very short day from Badminton in January 1946, just after the war. I arranged a special and unadvertised bye-day with a Meet near the house, but to our great disappointment, when we looked out of the windows that morning we were greeted by the sight of a white and frosty world. When I went out to study the state of the ground, I decided that it was just, but only just, soft enough to take hounds out. Nothing is worse for their feet than hard frost-bound ground, which can skin them completely and make them tender for weeks afterwards. Luckily a fox was found almost immediately, and the Princess was able to enjoy a short hunt across Little Badminton Farm and back into the Park.

Whatever previous royal precedents had been set, Queen Mary remained firmly loyal to her own main interests which were antique furniture and *objêts d'art* of which she had a world-renowned collection. However, quite apart from her outdoor forestry activities, her acute eye was not only for antique brass handles and Georgian snuffboxes. Urged on by constant reminders on the wireless, on posters and in the newspapers, and with the war effort always at the front of her mind, Queen Mary developed a similar and equally acquisitive taste for old bottles and scrap iron. To her delight, she often saw what she thought would help to swell her horde in the shape of field harrows and other farm implements that were left habitually and deliberately in the corners of fields by farmers, and were therefore out in all weather as there was nowhere else to store them. On Queen Mary's command, up would be swept these implements by her salvage corps, but the next morning, without her knowledge, they would be replaced quietly and tactfully so that nobody was any the wiser.

At the many local bazaars and sales of work that abounded during those years in aid of the War Effort, Queen Mary enjoyed looking after a stall, and she often took a turn serving tea in troop canteens. Nothing pleased her more than to attend the sing-songs and ENSA concerts that were laid on to entertain her guard in their quarters from time to time. Like us, all the Royal Family enjoy a sing-song, and we have had many happy evenings at

Badminton when one or other of them has been staying, raising the roof with our rendering of hunting songs. We always have a specially jolly party in March when Queen Elizabeth, The Queen Mother, comes to stay with us for the Cheltenham Race Festival.

Although we had had a roof reinforced to add to Queen Mary's safety in case of an air raid, she was nonetheless very reluctant to make use of it, preferring to remain in bed. However, when the danger became too great in the peak air-raid time of 1940, at three o'clock in the morning, soon after the air-raid sirens had wailed out their strident message, she was joined one by one by the other members of the household, usually still half-asleep and still in their nightclothes covered by hastily donned dressing-gowns; they found the Queen sitting bolt upright, already fully and immaculately dressed and working hard on *The Times* crossword puzzle.

On the fall of France in June 1940, when my wife's own younger brother, Frederick, was killed at Dunkirk, a move was made to persuade Queen Mary to return to Windsor Castle. However, by then she had settled at Badminton so well, that she made it clear that nothing short of the arrival of the German army would persuade her to shift from a place where she had not only made herself so popular, but had become personally so very happy and absorbed in all her doings.

The following little story is a tribute to her popularity. One day she dropped a handkerchief which was picked up by one of the young guards who was on duty outside. Not realising that he had been observed by Queen Mary from one of the windows, he put it in his pocket, intending to keep it as a souvenir. Later Queen Mary asked him for it back, and, very reluctantly, he had to produce it, only to be told that he was welcome to keep it. He sent it home to be framed, and no doubt it occupies a place of honour to this day.

When she had become really well-established at Badminton, Queen Mary took to regularly wearing the famous 'fore and aft' cap badge of the Gloucestershire Regiment from whom her guard were drawn and of which her son, the Duke of Gloucester, was Colonel-in-Chief.

At the end of August 1942, Queen Mary received news of the death of her son, the Duke of Kent, who was killed in a plane crash in Scotland when his own younger son, Prince Michael of Kent, was only six weeks old. Queen Mary insisted on attending his funeral at Windsor, this being one of only two visits she made to the Castle during her whole stay at Badminton, the other being for the confirmation of Princess Elizabeth. On her way back from the ordeal of her son's funeral, her car travelled through a terrible thunderstorm, and the ever-thoughtful Queen, on seeing some disconsolate figures, soaked to the skin, sheltering by the roadside, told her chauffeur to stop the car. She then opened the window and beckoned the young men to get in. So she made the acquaintance of two men whom she described as 'a charming young American parachutist, most friendly' and of 'a nice Sergeant Observer in the Air Force, who had taken part in the raid on Dieppe last week...'

Having once started to give lifts to servicemen, there was no stopping Queen Mary, and from that day onwards, her despatch riders and chauffeur were given emphatic orders that they must always be prepared to pick up young men – and women – in uniform who were thumbing a lift by the roadside.

I myself benefited from this habit of motorists stopping not only to give lifts, but also to help others, for when I was still in the army and on my way home to Badminton on urgent business, I had a puncture. Desperately I struggled with the jack and wrenched at the wheel brace in a vain attempt to loosen the nuts, but not a millimetre would they budge, and it was all too evident that this was a two-man job. Fortunately for me just as I was thinking of giving up in despair and joining the ranks of those who stand with thumb in air (and for the first time in my life rather wishing that I were a pretty girl instead of a middle-aged soldier), an Army convoy came into sight, and a staff car drew up by my side:

'Do you want some help, Sir?' came the question in a light voice with an unmistakable transatlantic accent that belied his British uniform.

'Oh, yes please,' I answered gratefully. 'I have to get back to Badminton as quickly as possible, and you can see for yourself what's happened.'

In what seemed like a brace of shakes, while I sat comfortably in the Commander's car sheltering from the rain that had been adding to my miseries, his men had bodily lifted up that car of mine, undone those damned nuts and fitted the spare wheel. I was able to drive on westwards towards Badminton with the minimum of delay, waving grateful thanks to the Commander over my shoulder as I went on my way. He was none other than David Niven, the film actor, who was to become a firm friend of mine from that day on.

In 1941 I heard that the Admiralty had had a burst of imagination and had named a class of destroyer that was coming into service against submarines the 'Hunt' class; one of them was called H.M.S. *Beaufort*. The Commanding Officer of this ship wrote to me on 1 July 1941 to give me the news, and in his letter he expressed the hope that his ship would be as famous for submarine hunting as my pack of hounds for fox-hunting!

When, in the spring of 1945, peace came to Europe at last, it was with genuine tears in her eyes that dear Queen Mary said goodbye to all of us and to Badminton, the house she had come to love nearly as much as we do. Her parting words were:

'Oh, I *have* been happy! Here I've been anybody to everybody, and back in London I shall have to start being Queen Mary all over again!'

This happy breed of men, this little world...
This blessed plot, this earth, this realm, this England.
[*Richard II*, Act II, Scene i, lines 45, 50.]

CHAPTER NINE

THE BADMINTON THREE-DAY EVENT

The most important sporting event that followed the end of World War II was the Olympic Games of 1948, when it was the turn of the United Kingdom to be the host country. The mounted competitions consisted of an individual Dressage competition, which, together with a Three-Day Horse-Trials Event, was held at Aldershot. A Show Jumping competition called the *Prix des Nations* was staged at Wembley, where the majority of the athletics and other competitions took place.

I went down to Aldershot to watch the individual Dressage competition, and the following day I saw our team competing the first leg of the Horse-Trials Event. After having seen the individual displays by competitors from nine countries, which produced some of the finest spectacles of horsemanship that it had up to then ever been my pleasure to enjoy, it was with a sense of anti-climax that I watched our own team, Major P. Borwick on Liberty, Brigadier Lyndon Bolton on Sylvester, and Major D. Stewart on Dark Seal, as they competed against the crack European teams. Their disappointingly poor performances made it only too evident that unless a proper training programme were carried out, we might as well abandon all idea of competing in the international field, for our Dressage was farcical when it was compared with the polished performances given by the continental competitors. However, the following day we somewhat vindicated ourselves in the Cross Country section, when Major Borwick on Liberty rode a wonderful round. Even so, Brigadier Lyndon Bolton had two falls, and finally the whole team was eliminated when Major Stewart's horse was found to be lame and had to be pulled up right at the start.

Fortunately we showed that British horses and riders are

capable of great things by coming third in the *Prix des Nations* Show Jumping competition at Wembley, against very strong competition.

But it was when I stood at Aldershot watching the efforts of our team with a deepening sense of gloom, that the germ of an idea came into my mind. What a good thing it would be, I thought, if a competition run on exactly the same lines as the Olympic Horse Trials could be held each year in this country. This would serve to provide British horses and riders with the impetus, the encouragement and the experience it was self-evident they so badly needed. For when compared with their international counterparts, the British team seemed to be a bunch of amateurs who relied on an army training to carry them through what was a very professional affair. They were pitting themselves against opponents who quite obviously spent a large part of the year training and competing on horses that had been very carefully selected for the job.

As I sat munching my picnic lunch, I thought to myself that with our well-earned international reputation not only for breeding fine horses, but also for producing courageous, skilful riders in the hunting and show-jumping fields, surely to goodness the time had now come when we must do something concrete to ensure that we were able to produce a really well-trained team of horses and riders to send to Helsinki for the Olympic Games four years hence. I came to the firm conclusion that if stringent efforts were not made immediately, it would be better for us to stay away from Finland altogether, as far as the Olympic Horse Trials were concerned, if we did not wish to make ourselves the laughing-stock of the international horse world.

So I made a tentative suggestion that a Three-Day Event should be held in my Park at Badminton the following year. Little did I think that this suggestion would be taken up in such a whole-hearted way, not only by the British Horse Society and would-be members of a future British team, but also by the general public. My idea snowballed so quickly that I really felt quite bewildered. The British Horse Society undertook to run the event and they have done so ever since. They benefit from all the profits which are put towards part of the expense of training future Olympic teams, and also towards the cost of sending British teams of show-jumpers all over the world, teams that have competed successfully for many years. The British Horse Society not only do these things, but they concern themselves with a host of other tremendously worthwhile activities that help to foster and maintain country-wide interest in horses.

To show their appreciation of my hospitality at Badminton over the years, the British Horse Society have built me a magnificent covered riding school – a building that was sadly lacking in my stable complex which has changed very little since the last row of horse-boxes was completed by my grandfather in 1880. Not only will this be an invaluable adjunct to my stables, but I hope that it will provide the venue for a host of activities throughout the year, and I am sure it will prove to be an invaluable asset at the time of the Horse Trials each year.

The name Badminton has now become synonymous, not only with a pack of hounds and an indoor game, but also with what are now known as the Badminton Horse Trials. The expression 'Three-Day Event' had been dropped by 1950, though I must admit that in our family we have never called it anything else. In the beginning, it was a very amateurish affair, with the Dressage competition taking place on the old cricket pitch in front of the house. In those early years, the atmosphere was rather like that of a pleasant cross between a private garden party where there was mounted entertainment, and a point-to-point meeting. People perched on the straw bales that delineated the extent of the dressage arena, and happy picnic parties sat around watching the competition.

However, in 1959, torrential rain turned the whole area into a sea of mud, so a new site had to be found well away from the house. Numbers of spectators that could be counted in thousands that first year, very soon became tens of thousands; nowadays it is estimated that something like a quarter of a million people crowd to my Park to enjoy those four or five days in April.

The whole thing has changed out of all recognition from the early days; now, weeks ahead an army of workmen arrives with dozens of lorry-loads of scaffolding which they erect round a large area to the north-west of the house, turning it into a vast arena surrounded by covered stands. Not only that, but they also put up a large complex of tented shops that do a roaring trade throughout the Horse Trials. These shops attract customers from far and wide, who find that not only can they re-equip themselves and their horses at the end of the hunting season and the outset of the showing one, but they can also furnish their houses, buy food, lay in wine, and buy jokes with which to trick their friends. Then, when they feel the need for refreshment, they are able to sink exhausted into chairs and sip the free drinks that are provided by the banks that tour the country with their travelling stands, visiting all the big agricultural shows.

On looking back with the inevitable wisdom of hindsight, I now realise that my bright idea could well have turned out to be a crazy one that would have served to disrupt the whole of my estate.

To a large extent, it is thanks to the co-operation and help of all the workers on my estate, led by my agent, Tim Mitchell, that the venture was able to prosper and to become the undoubted success that it is. Tim Mitchell says quite firmly that our farming is done around the Three-Day Event. We leave the big fields that are used as car parks down to grass, and later in the summer they serve to provide me with the enormous amount of hay that is needed at Badminton. My horses, of which I keep a large number, eat hay, but so do my two herds of Shorthorns and another of Guernseys, as well as my store-cattle. We also have to feed our deer during the hardest of the winter months.

In the first instance, we formed a British Horse Society Committee of which I was President, and the chair was taken by Colonel the Hon. Guy Cubitt, who was then also Chairman of the British Horse Society and one of the most fervent protagonists of the Pony Club. It was not long before it became clear that we would need to have a local Committee as well, this one composed of people living in or around Badminton, and therefore in a position to deal with all the day-to-day issues that inevitably crop up.

The first Director of the Badminton Three-Day Event was Colonel Trevor Horn, a founder member of the British Horse Society, who had discovered himself pitch-forked from a place on the Selection Committee for the 1948 Olympic Three-Day Event into being Arena Manager for the Grand Prix de Dressage and the Three-Day-Event Dressage at Aldershot, and also for the Show Jumping *Grand Prix des Nations* that followed at Wembley.

Poor Colonel Horn was given only two weeks before those Olympic Games in which to prepare himself and to learn all that he could in such a short time about the practical running of such an event, with all its attendant complexities. He put up a splendid show, although he had only had a very limited experience when he came to Badminton. He more than made up for his lack of experience by his abundant wealth of enthusiasm.

It soon became quite a common sight for me at Badminton when I went out and about in the Park, to come across Colonel Horn riding his bicycle armed with a wheel measurer as he planned the layout of the course and the design of the fences. Nowadays the whole business of both Eventing and Show Jumping have become so high-powered, that a new profession has come into being during the course of the last twenty years – that of course-builder. People who take up this highly skilled job find themselves involved in course-building for Eventing and very complex Show Jumping layouts all over the world, in which every millimetre is of vital importance.

Back in those far-off days in the 1950s, when we all took the thing so light-heartedly, I used to love to try out all the fences myself as they were being built. I felt that if my best hunter could clear them, then they would surely be good enough for the eventers and would provide a sufficient challenge. I don't think I'd care to take on some of the fences nowadays, since they have become increasingly stiff as general standards have risen.

In the early days, the spectators were free to go wherever they liked as long as they didn't actually get on to the course when the competition was taking place. But as their numbers have swelled, it has been found necessary to erect barriers around the fences so that the competitors are not hindered in their progress. The barriers are intended not only for the safety of the horses and their riders, but are also designed to safeguard the spectators.

We have a mounted band of volunteers drawn from my own Hunt and also from our neighbouring ones; their duty is to act as stewards. They stand guard at each jump and blow a whistle when they get a signal that another competitor is coming, so warning the spectators to clear the course. Split-second timing is an essential part of successful Eventing, and a small delay or hold-up of any kind could well prove catastrophic to a competitor. This band of volunteers – and it is quite a large one – is ruled over in an apparently benevolent way by my Joint Master, Gerald Gundry, whose tact is only matched by his charm – but believe me, that glove of velvet covers a truly strong hand.

Some of the horses are inevitably going to come to grief, so an elaborate system of signals and messages comes into operation; should a horse be cast into one of the ditches or straddle one of the fences, it is possible to hold up the oncoming competitors. Each jump is tied together with rope so that if a horse does get caught in this way it can be swiftly freed. An axe is placed in a strategic position by each fence to be used to demolish it if necessary by the officials responsible for each one. Once demolished, it then has to be rebuilt again as quickly as possible in order to cause the minimum of delay.

Local Pony Clubs also supply bands of young people who, mounted on their own ponies, fetch and carry messages. The Pony Club serves a dual purpose in the Eventing world, for it provides our future would-be Eventers with a wonderful background of training, combined with the necessary experience and enthusiasm. The members of our winning team at the Munich Olympics in 1972 were all members of one or another of the Pony Clubs attached to their local Hunts, proof in itself of the value of the movement.

One of the other factors that had a strong bearing on my original decision to invite people to come and use my Park in this way for a Three-Day Event was that I knew I would be able to provide adequate stabling for all the horses. By the time the Trials take place towards the end of April, most of my own hunters have been turned away for a well-deserved holiday out at grass, except for the two or three we keep up for my hunt staff to ride at the Horse Trials when they form part of Gerald Gundry's team of stewards, and during the summer when they take my hounds to parade at various Horse Shows and other money-raising occasions round and about the country.

By the time the middle of April is reached it is fairly easy to predict how many competitors there will be, as out of a very large entry a good many will have dropped out for one reason or another, and the final number is usually between seventy and eighty.

Since that first Badminton in 1949, the Horse Trials have been held each year in my Park, save for 1955 when, at the express wish of the Queen, they were held at Windsor Great Park in conjunction with the European Championship. Alas, in 1963, 1966 and 1975 they were rained off.

As the whole thing went from strength to strength, the overall standard of our team continued to improve under the training of Tony Collings of Porlock Weir, who was tragically killed in the first Comet air crash in 1952.

That giant among men, my old friend, Lt Colonel Sir Michael (Mike) Ansell must also take his fair share, and more, of praise, for without his guidance and enthusiasm, the pattern of British competitive equestrianism may well have been quite different. I will quote Lt Colonel Sir Harry Llewellyn, a member of the winning British Show Jumping team in the *Grand Prix des Nations* at Helsinki in 1952:

> ... But above all, we have had the great strength of our Chairman, Mike Ansell, always behind us. In his presence we have never dared lose a Nations Cup!
>
> When the last British horse had jumped and the issue was clear, a wild figure was seen which appeared to have ten wind-milling arms and as many legs. Many people trained their glasses on this phenomenon only to discover that it was our inspiration in everything – MIKE ANSELL.

What makes it seem incredible is the fact that Mike was blinded by enemy action during the last war. He was injured and taken prisoner by the Germans, and the damage sustained by his eyes necessitated very delicate operations. I am happy to say that not only did the German authorities willingly undertake to arrange these, but Mike is still friendly with the German surgeon who carried them out. In spite of all the care that was taken, those delicate operations were not successful, and so Mike is permanently blind. However, he is not a man to sit down and bow his head under such an affliction. As soon as he returned to this country after the war, he started to plan the courses at the International Horse Show, which in those days was held at the White City. He was its efficient secretary for many years, and I its proud President. We had many happy weeks both at the White City and then at Wembley where it moved when access to the White City became difficult owing to a complex layout of motorways in its vicinity.

There must have been few horse-lovers who were not familiar with the sight of that tall figure going out into the ring, his hand resting lightly on someone's shoulder, on his way to make sure for himself that everything was absolutely in order. You can take it for granted that the Show would not have continued unless everything was, for Mike is a perfectionist. Even now, he supervises the forestry on his Devon Estate, in spite of the fact that he has had no sight for thirty-five years, and even opens his garden to the public. What an example he is to us all!

The culmination of those early days at Badminton was when

Great Britain, with a team consisting of Lt Colonel Frank Weldon, late of the King's Troop, the Royal Horse Artillery, (who was later destined to become Director of the Badminton Horse Trials) riding Kilbarry, Major Lawrence Rook riding Wild Venture, and a young hitherto unknown farmer from Devon, Bertie Hill, riding Countryman III, won the Team Event at the Stockholm Olympic Games in 1956. They scored –335.48 points, beating their runners-up, Germany, by a hundred and forty points.

The exciting week at Badminton always begins with the 'Vetting'. This takes place in my stableyard, where a large crowd of people collect to watch the horses being put through their paces and examined by a team of Veterinary Surgeons. All the horses are inspected before the competition begins, and at set times throughout to make sure they are fit to continue. Obviously it is essential that the horses should be passed A-1, not only for their own safety, but also for that of their riders.

The next two days are devoted to the Dressage tests, when all the competitors are called upon to do a complicated performance in front of three separate judges of international repute and different nationalities, their marking being done quite independently – rather in the same way as the World Skating Championships and the 'Miss World' competitions that attract such a large television public.

For this section of the event, the dress of the competitor has to be formal; it is amazing how smart they manage to look, considering that the majority of them are living in caravans. The horses must be as impeccably turned out as their riders.

Saturday is the day for the speed and endurance phase of the competition, the day of the spectacular performances, so it is also the day when vast numbers of horse enthusiasts flock to Badminton to watch the thrills and the spills, and perhaps to enjoy a vicarious pleasure as they watch the brilliant performances of some of the young competitors. This is the day when the local police forces find themselves strained to the utmost as they are called upon to deal with the thousands of cars that come flooding into Badminton village and my Park from all points of the compass. Crawling along, nose to tail, they fill all the little lanes for miles around, even causing hold-ups and delays as far afield as the M4 Motorway. There are three Police Forces concerned, Avon, Gloucestershire and Wiltshire, and the whole operation is a masterpiece of co-ordination.

Although naturally I myself have never had any personal experience of the traffic conditions, I am told that nowadays the whole thing runs like clockwork so that eventually all the vehicles find themselves parked up in or around the environs of the Park. We set aside a section for disabled drivers, placing this by what we consider is likely to be one of the more interesting and difficult jumps which will provide those people who are unable to leave their cars with an exciting day's viewing.

Crowds collect around all the jumps, the most dense one tending to be by the water jump at the far end of the Park Pond – the original source of Badminton's water supply. Here the horses are required to jump into the water, wade for a few strides, and then leap an obstacle built on the bank to get out on to dry ground again. Seldom does a day go by without someone getting a wetting, which gives great pleasure to the crowd of spectators. Just as events are only newsworthy when things go wrong, people tend to enjoy the misfortunes of others. Do not think for a moment that I am saying that people come to Badminton in order to see the competitors take a fall. Of course they don't; they come to see equine performance at its most superb, and great big splashes just add to the fun of the whole day.

I don't think anybody enjoys the week more than I do. I love to go round the shops, which are many and varied, and I always make a point of accompanying the Queen, who has come to Badminton to stay with us for the Three-Day Event for many years now, on a tour that takes in the shops as well as a round tour of the fences in my Land-Rover. The course is different each year. Not only are the fences different, but the course is taken from left to right one year and from right to left the following one.

Recently, the Queen has had an added interest when she visits Badminton, for two of her own family have been competing. Captain Mark Phillips has been the winner three times, twice on his aunt's, Miss Flavia Phillips, horse, Great Ovation, and once on the Queen's own horse, Columbus. Princess Anne has competed several times, and has also been in the prize money. I think it says a lot both for her courage and for her determination that Princess Anne has managed to get to the top in such a competitive field, in spite of, rather than because of, her background and position. Once in the saddle of a spiritsome, agile and fit horse, it matters not a jot what the antecedents of a rider are – all that matters is that he or she should have a stout heart and a fit body, combined with a high degree of skill that will enable them to make the sustained effort required to carry them through to the end of the gruelling three days, where victory may or may not be waiting.

In his excellent book, *The Royal Office of Master of the Horse*, M. M. Reese says in the introduction: '. . . The office [of Master of the Horse] has usually been most solid and secure and successful when the incumbent and the Sovereign have shared a personal interest in horses and have been able to ride them.'

I wholeheartedly agree with him, and there can be few people better qualified than I am to state categorically that there can have been no Monarch in the whole history of these islands who has been a more keen supporter of all forms of equitation than our present Queen. She is herself an accomplished horsewoman, and there are not many people who have a more comprehensive knowledge of bloodstock and racing. The Queen has a photographic memory for horses, especially for those she has bred herself. I am told that once she has seen one of her own foals, she will then unerringly be able to pick it out from a host of others, in spite of the fact that within the course of a few weeks the animal may have completely changed its appearance. When she pays one of her regular visits to her studs, she waves away notebooks and photographs, relying entirely on her own memory, needing neither props nor prompting.

Her enthusiasm for horses is shared by most of her family; the Duke of Edinburgh, after a successful career as a polo player, has now reached international standards as an amateur whip in coaching competitions. In 1971, after her great performances in the Eventing field, Princess Anne was voted 'Sportswoman of the Year', and Prince Charles, the Prince of Wales, is as keen a polo player as ever his father was. He is also an ardent rider to hounds, much to my own delight, for it was I who first introduced him to the sport several years ago. I am proud to say that when he comes out with my hounds he wears my Blue and Buff. Recently, following in the footsteps of his uncle, the Duke of Windsor when he was Prince of Wales, Prince Charles has taken to the arduous sport of steeple-chasing.

Before ever they come to Badminton, all the competitors need to have reached a peak of physical fitness, though they say that the sheer physical effort of schooling several horses keeps them in hard condition. In addition to fitness of body, a rider also needs courage and an ability to think fast; these qualities must be combined with an unflappable temperament and a great capacity for concentration. Believe me, nothing affects the behaviour of a horse more quickly than any sign of hesitation or lack of nerve. They seem to be gifted with some sort of extrasensory perception that instantly tells them the exact state of their rider's mind. Should there be any defect, you may be sure that the horse will quickly take advantage of it, either becoming nervous or behaving in as diabolical way as possible. It will seem to take a positive delight in dropping a shoulder at a crucial moment, off-loading its rider and then galloping off. Everyone who hunts has had this sort of experience at one time or another, and if they deny it, then I am afraid they are not being truthful. You can fool all of the people some of the time, you can fool some of the people all of the time, but you can never fool your horse!

Frank Weldon, who has designed the course at Badminton for many years now, says quite frankly that his aim is to frighten the living daylights out of the riders when they are on their feet, but at the same time to build jumps that are perfectly possible for horses that are of Olympic calibre. The Three-Day Event, while testing a horse's ability in almost every sort of equine movement and activity of which a horse is capable, at the same time aims to provide a comprehensive test of all-round horsemanship.

The competition is scored throughout on a penalty basis: in other words, marks are taken away for faults, and are not added for good performance. The marks awarded by the Dressage judges, for instance, are converted into penalties by being subtracted from the maximum number of points it is possible to score. On the second day, the Speed and Endurance Test is decided on a combination of time and jumping ability, the time laid down for each phase being calculated on the speeds, which under the scoring system that used to be in force, would have earned horse and rider what was then called 'maximum bonus'. This means that if the phase is completed within what they call the Optimum Time, then the competitor incurs no penalty – in other words, if a competitor completes the course within the time limit, he or she can score full marks, providing there have been no mistakes made at the obstacles. There are 'Jump Judges' at every fence who assess the performance of each horse and rider.

The same system of marking applies to the Jumping Test which takes place in the main arena on the final day, and the outright winner is the combination of horse and rider that have incurred the least number of penalties in all three days. Should by any chance two competitors finish the jumping with the same score, then the winner is determined by taking the best cross-country marks.

The Dressage Test serves the dual purpose of limbering the horse up for the cross-country test the next day, while at the same time showing that it is capable of the very controlled movements that are required of it – a form of equine eurhythmics. A horse needs to be quiet and obedient, moving with grace and accuracy, while maintaining the sort of presence that catches the eye. If a horse is fit enough to do the cross-country course, then it will be far fitter than those kept only for Dressage purposes, and will therefore be much more of a handful and far more difficult to keep in a quiet and obedient frame of mind. So the rider of a horse that performs really well in the Dressage section of the Three-Day Event is more especially to be commended.

The following day begins with a course of roads and tracks where the time allowed means that a competitor needs to maintain a speed that might be described as a sort of scout's pace, a mixture of a canter and a walk. It is very important to keep an eye on the time, and a series of numbered kilometre markers are put up at strategic places so that competitors can keep checking their speed with a stop watch; some of them wear a watch on each wrist: one to give an over-all time at a glance, and the other to check the time taken for individual parts of the course.

The next section is a steeplechase course, with fences of the type that are normally used for point-to-points. This is where speed and stamina come into the picture, for up to then the emphasis has mainly been on grace and control of movement. Here again, time is all-important, as the aim is to complete this course in precisely five minutes, no more and no less, and this means averaging about 26 m.p.h. (about 43 kilometres an hour). No advantage is gained by getting in earlier; although an early arrival is not penalised, it can prove to put a horse at a severe disadvantage. By going too fast, it may well have lost some of the vital energy it is going to need so desperately and that should therefore be carefully conserved for the real endurance test that follows later in the day when it is faced with Frank Weldon's cross-country course.

The steeplechase course is followed by a further short section of roads and tracks, this time of six miles or ten kilometres. While the general conditions of the competition are exactly the same as in the first one, the horse's behaviour will not be. He may well be blowing and sweating after his gallop, and will therefore need to be nursed along. Indeed, many riders dismount and run alongside their horse to relieve it of their weight, this behaviour coming within the rules; even so, there can be no respite, as the clock will tick on relentlessly, and there are severe time penalties for late arrival.

At the end of this section, there is then a very welcome and much-needed ten-minute break before the competitors embark on the cross-country course. This is the time when the rider tries to relax while the veterinary surgeons are inspecting his horse. There will be a chance to ask how other people have been getting on and to find out as much as possible about the state of the going. Eventing is one sport when it is a positive disadvantage to go first, however enticing may be the thought of getting the thing over and done with. In the light of the information received, each rider will then be able to plan their own approach to the obstacles, and, having already walked the course and studied the jumps several times, they can map out in their minds which way each fence should be taken. These decisions will be made in the light of the prevailing weather conditions, the state of the ground, and also the condition of each individual horse and its own particular ability at certain types of fence.

The main object of the test is to jump the obstacles successfully, but at the same time it is necessary to maintain a gruelling speed in order to do so within the severe time limits that are set; this speed will vary from horse to horse. Some obstacles will need to be taken fairly slowly by all the competitors, but at others it is really safer to take them fast thus allowing the horse to spread itself in order to clear the ditch that may be on the other side. The rider will know about this, but of course the horse will be totally unaware of it. The rider has to be the final judge of the varying speeds at which to take each fence, and the decision is made by assessing the joint abilities of horse and rider.

Between the jumps a relentless gallop must be maintained if time penalties are to be avoided altogether, but the fact is that the actual speed at each individual obstacle is what will decide the ultimate outcome. It has to be constantly borne in mind that, while a horse must be taken at its maximum speed, not only must it have enough energy left in hand to finish the course that day, but also sufficient to complete the Show Jumping course on the following day.

On that final day, competitors have to be up with the lark to give their horses a gentle work-out which will loosen them up before the compulsory veterinary examination. Although the Sunday course looks like a simple show jumping one, there is more to it than that, and, here again, small mistakes are severely penalised. After the gruelling conditions of the Saturday programme, a horse's reactions are bound to be a little slower than usual, and its spring may be a lot less. Skill and experience in the Show Jumping ring are bound to be useful assets, but the way the horse was ridden the previous day ultimately decides what performance the horse is likely to make.

Throughout the whole competition, the strength and courage of the horse have to be matched by the rider, whose spirit and tact, combined with grit, determination and good judgement are the factors needed for success.

To my mind, success does not only mean winning. I think that horse and rider can consider themselves successful if they manage to complete the whole competition.

The preparations for the Three-Day Event at Badminton itself are seemingly endless; now a full-time office has been set up in the village to deal with the mass of work that has to be carried out long before the great Event comes along.

My own programme has to take into account the fact that we always have a number of members of the Royal Family staying in the House, and naturally I make it my business to see that their stay is as enjoyable as possible. To this end, we give dinner parties each night, often with an entertainment on the last one to which we invite as many as possible of the people who have given so freely of their time and energies in one capacity or other to help to make the whole thing run smoothly.

On the Saturday, I have to keep to a fairly fixed timetable, for naturally what the Queen wants to see above all is Princess Anne or Captain Mark Phillips taking as many jumps as possible. To this end, I take her in my Land-Rover (which has had a special clean to get rid of all the dog hairs) and lead a procession of Land-Rovers and Range-Rovers around the course.

Naturally, whenever the Queen moves about there have to be security precautions, but she herself always 'pooh poohs' the idea of any danger, and is quite prepared to do a 'walk-about'. Although the crowds come in the main to watch the competition, there is no doubt that most of them have the thought in mind that they may be fortunate enough to catch a glimpse of the Queen. I have farm wagons placed at strategic points along the course from which my Royal visitors are able to see above the heads of the crowd, though very often they choose to sit on the grass just inside the barriers.

On the Sunday morning we attend a special service in our Church, and then, after an early luncheon, we get into the collection of Land- and Range-Rovers again and drive across from the house to the big arena at the far end. After circling it very slowly, the vehicles pull up in front of the west stand where a section is roped off to form a Royal Box.

There is a great deal of excitement and tension, as the surviving entrants come into the ring to parade before the start of the final and deciding test, especially if two or three competitors lie very close together.

The one carrying the most penalty points jumps first, and so it continues, until the final jump made by the last competitor decides the result of the whole competition. What a thrill it must be to win at Badminton!

For most Eventing enthusiasts, the whole thing is over when the result of the Horse Trials is known and the prize-giving ceremony has taken place, although the afternoon's programme continues with a Show Jumping competition for all-comers.

The applause dies down as the Queen's entourage sweeps slowly around the ring again and away, and then the crowds start to disperse. Off they go to their homes in all corners of the British Isles to wait for another year, when I sincerely hope they will all come again to my park and take a share in all the thrills and excitement of yet another Badminton Three-Day Event.

*33. Members of the Royal Family at the Three-Day
Event in 1962. I wonder if Princess Anne already had
ideas of competing at Badminton.*

34. *We always have a special service in the Church during the Three-Day Event, when we generally invite a Bishop to preach.*

35. With some of my young hound bitches.

36. With some of my red deer stags that are standing
by the Park Pond, November 1980.

EPILOGUE

The wild life of to-day is not ours to dispose of as we please. We have it in trust. We must account for it to those who come after.

(King George VI)

Ninety years ago . . . on Wednesday evening the Lord Mayor entertained the members of the Beaufort Hunt at a banquet at the Mansion House, the evening being as unique as it was interesting . . . The Lord Mayor in proposing the toast of the evening, thanked the Duke of Beaufort and his son, the Marquess of Worcester, for the splendid way in which they had promoted the good old English pastime of Foxhunting in the Badminton country, and maintained that His Grace was as good a landlord, neighbour and politician as he was a sportsman . . . 'The Masters of Other Hounds,' given by the Lord Mayor, was responded to by the Earl of Cork, who said that whereas at the beginning of the century there were only about 25 packs in the country, at present there were no less than 150 and the increase showed that hunting was advancing in favour with all classes. He believed that, no matter what political party was in power, so long as foxhunting existed the country would flourish. (Laughter and cheers.)

(*Horse and Hound*, 7 June 1974)

At a British Field Sports Society dinner that was held at the Mansion House in the summer of 1980, I resigned from the Presidentship of that body. The aims of the British Field Sports

Society are so much in line with what I have always thought, believed in and striven towards all my life, that I think a resumé of the speech I made on that occasion would serve as a very fitting epilogue to this book of memoirs.

In a series of notebooks – they might perhaps be described as scrapbooks – that I kept during the post office strike some years ago, I have come across a page on which there are a couple of texts for hunting sermons.

The first of these is taken from the Book of the Prophet Isaiah, Chapter 62, Verse 10, and it reads:

Go through, go through the gates: prepare ye the way of the people; cast up, cast up the highway; gather out the stones; lift up a standard for the people.

The other is taken from my favourite Psalm, the hundred and twenty-first:

I will lift up mine eyes unto the hills from whence cometh my help.

Those of you who hunt – and there must be many such people here – indeed, on looking round, I can see many familiar faces of old hunting friends, will understand how easy it would be to base a sermon on either of those two texts.

On the opposite page of those note books I find that I have pasted in a table plan of a Banquet in honour of my grandfather held by the Lord Mayor of London, Sir Robert Fowler, in this very room here at the Mansion House on 4 June 1884, nearly a hundred years ago.

On looking at the list of people who sat at the top table, I see the names of many of my own family, including that of my great-aunt who was responsible for inventing the game of Badminton in our front hall when she was a child. We still have her battledore – home-made with great ingenuity. . . .

Another name I see is that of Lord Lonsdale, the celebrated Yellow Earl, who was not only a fine sportsman but he was also my Godfather.

Then there was the Earl of Cork who was Master of the Queen's Buckhounds, a job that would have fallen to my lot as Master of the Horse had I been born in an earlier reign. In mediaeval days, the Master of the

Horse was not only the Master of all the various packs of hounds that belonged to the King, but he also had to be responsible for the Royal Menagerie which was housed for hundreds of years in the Tower of London, and he was required to provide meat for the resident tiger.

Among those celebrated names were those also of Lord and Lady Trafalgar, he being the heir to Lord Nelson, nephew of the great Admiral. I note also that Mr and Mrs Clutterbuck were seated opposite to the *Standard*, the *Daily Telegraph* and the *Morning Post*.

So it is singularly appropriate that this wonderful feast – and I choose the word deliberately, as it is the one used so often for sporting dinners – should be held in these illustrious surroundings.

I must just tell you that Sir Robert Fowler, the Lord Mayor of 1884, used to arrive once a week at Paddington dressed in hunting clothes and brought there by the Lord Mayor's Coach. He then used to catch a train going west, enjoy a day's hunting with my father, and then return the way he had come!

I am truly grateful not only to the British Field Sports Society for arranging it all, but to the Lord Mayor, Sir Peter Gadsden, for extending his hospitality to us all. I am sure you would all want to join with me in offering our heartfelt thanks.

My grandfather, in whose honour that feast of so long ago was held, said that there could be no sport without controversy, and how true and prophetical his words have proved to be. Since then we have fought – and won – two world wars for our right to be free. Now all we want is to be able to enjoy our field sports without any interference from people who often, more's the pity, do not in the least understand what it is that they are opposing. They are fed with a mass of propaganda about the suffering of the poor little animals, without knowing anything about the discipline, skill and knowledge that is brought to bear in the realm of Field Sports – and those Field Sports are part of our heritage, every bit as much as are all the fine buildings that many of us fight hard to preserve. They are not so much sports as a dedicated way of life.

No body of people has fought harder than the British Field Sports Society of which I have had the great honour of being President since its instigation to preserve our right to conserve, using the methods that have been proved throughout several generations to be the best way of doing the job, in the same way as our forefathers.

Now I am stepping aside, and I use that phrase deliberately, as I feel that the time has come for a change. By saying 'step aside' I want to make it clear that I shall always have the interests of the British Field Sports Society at heart, and will always do everything in my power to promote its cause – and I will even go so far as to preach to the unconverted every time I come across one of those poor heathen.

May all the sports to which we have been lucky enough to be born, flourish and continue unmolested for ever, so that in another hundred years perhaps a kinsman of mine may stand here at a similar dinner singing the praises of the Society, and declaring that although Field Sports will always have to be defended, they still exist, and we are still free to choose what we will do with our leisure time.

The sun descending in the west,
The evening star does shine;
The birds are silent in their nest
And I must seek for mine.

INDEX

NB: for illustrations see list on p. viii

PHOTOGRAPHIC ACKNOWLEDGEMENTS

The publishers are grateful to the Duke of Beaufort for kindly making available material to be photographed at Badminton House and to Derek Balmer for taking the photographs, with the exception of the following:
BBC Hulton Picture Library, London 9; Camera Press, London 34; Central Press Photos, London 29, 32, 33; Country Life, London 14, 17; Hamlyn Group Picture Library, 16, 21; Imperial War Museum, London 31; Jim Meads, Westbury 27; Popperfoto, London 28; Sport and General Press Agency, London 30.